# The Islands of Magic

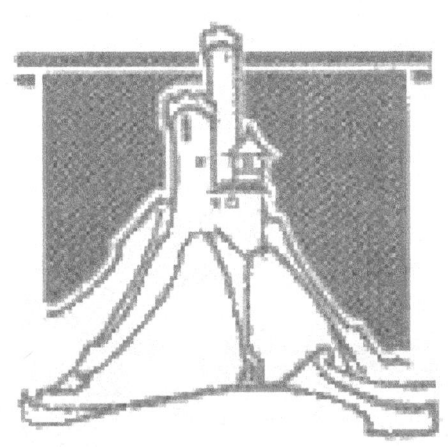

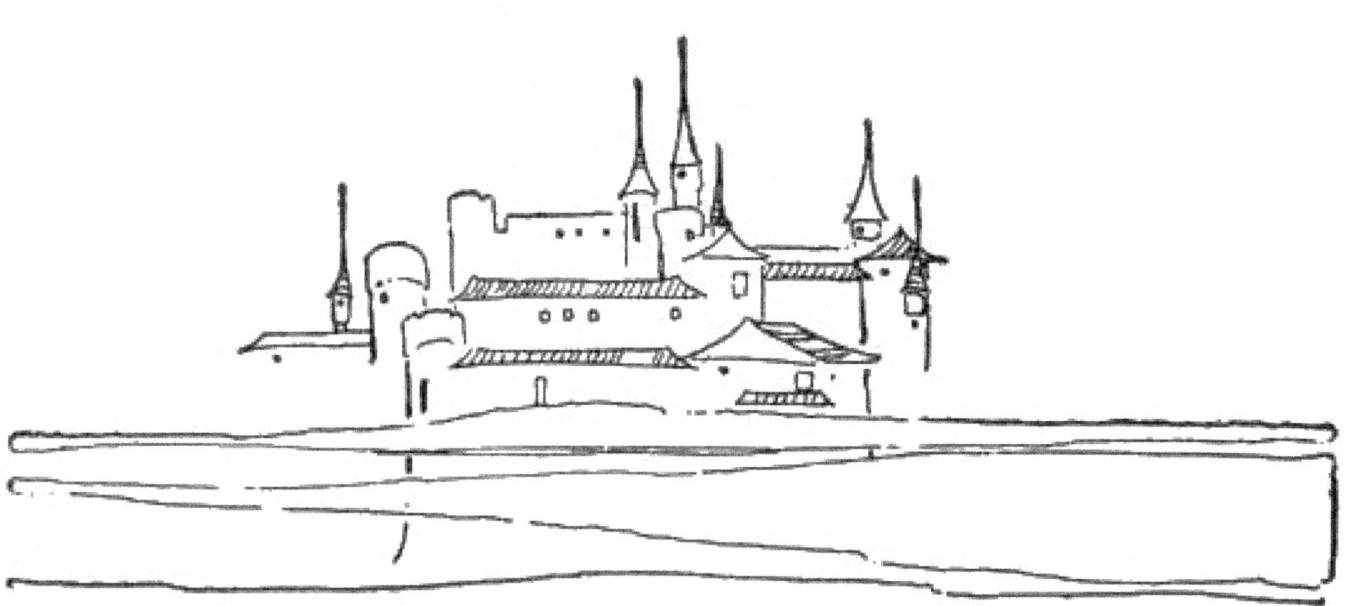

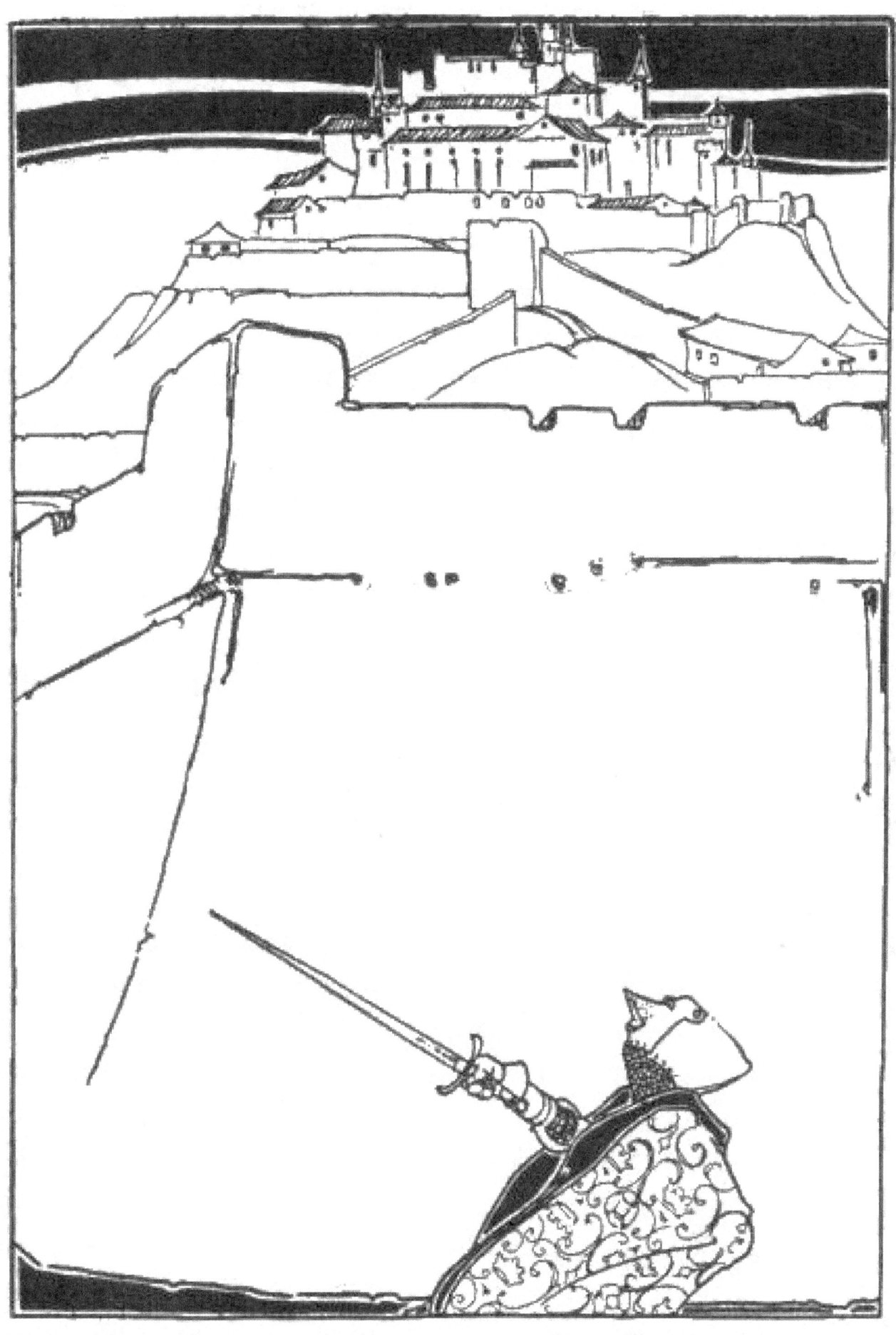

King Graywhite struck his royal sword against the great wall

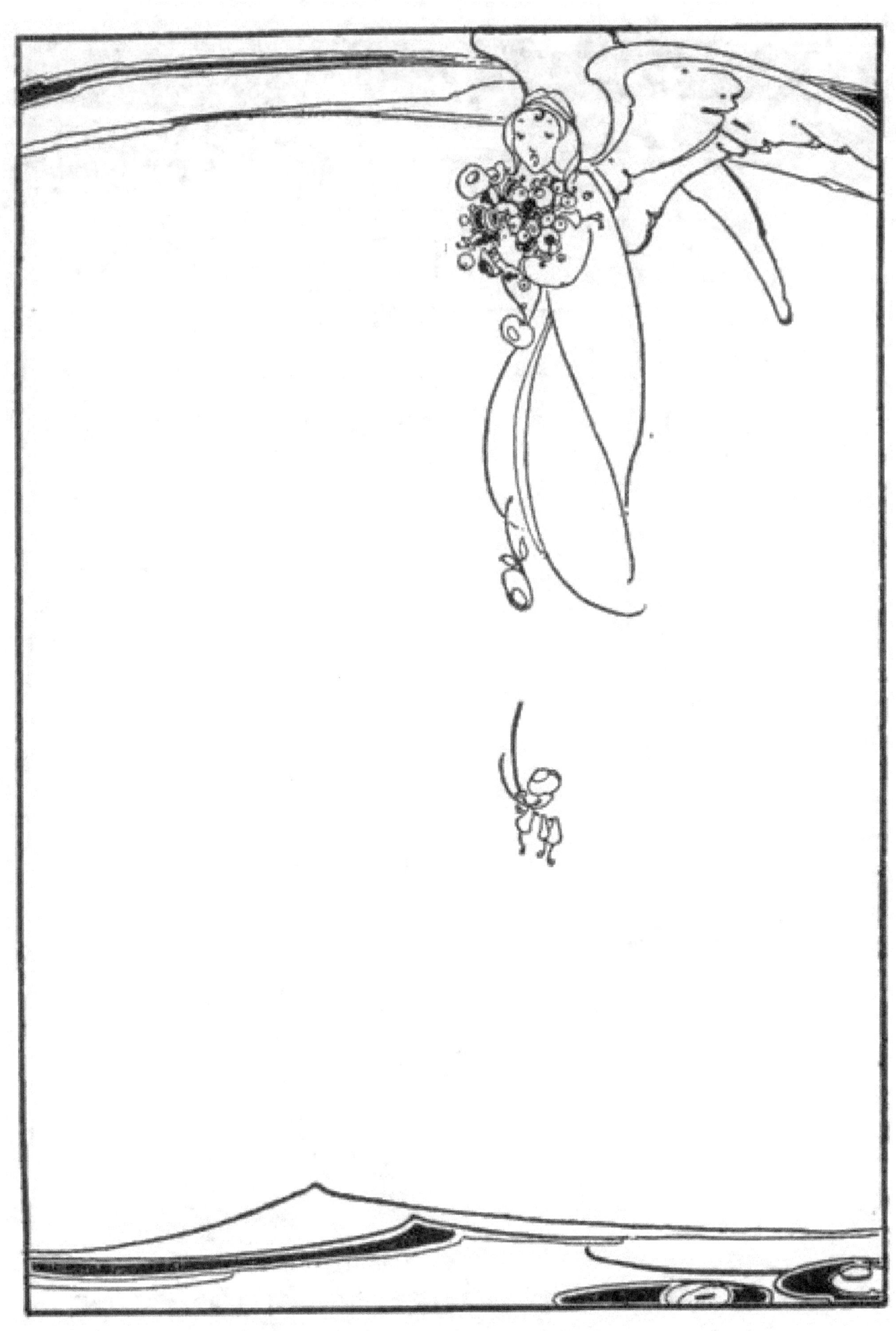

She could not hold them all

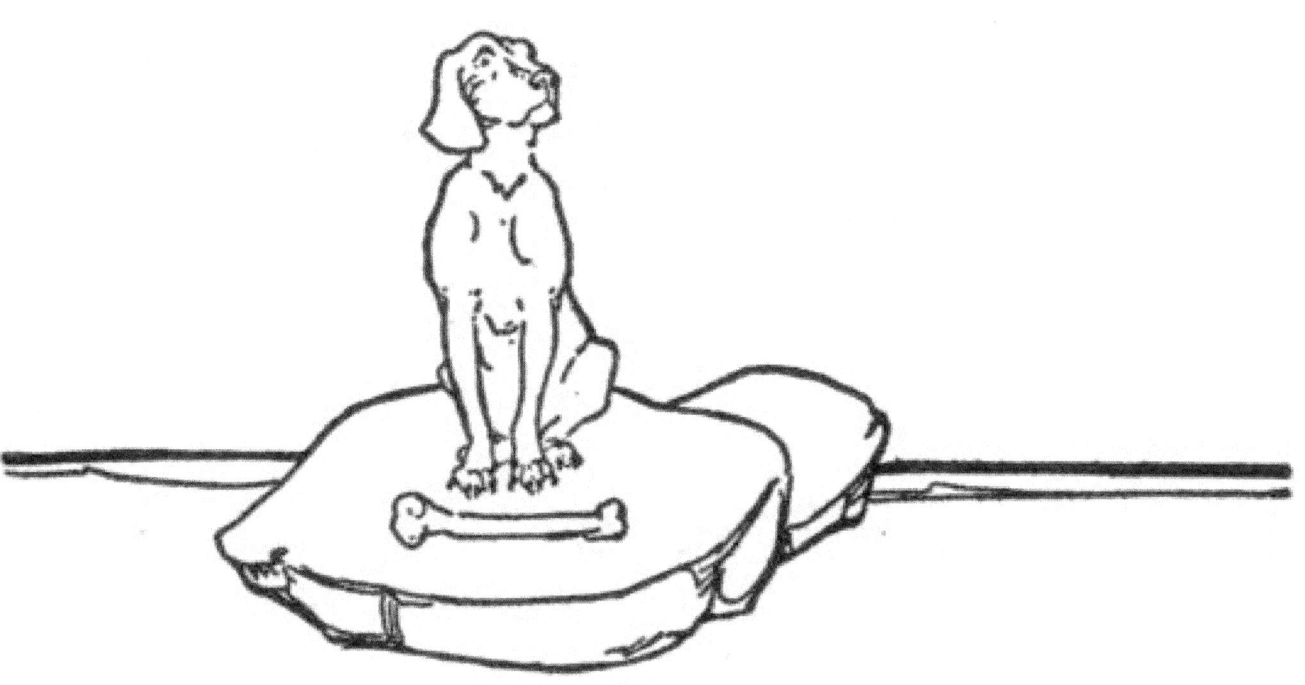

"Will somebody please pass the pepper?"

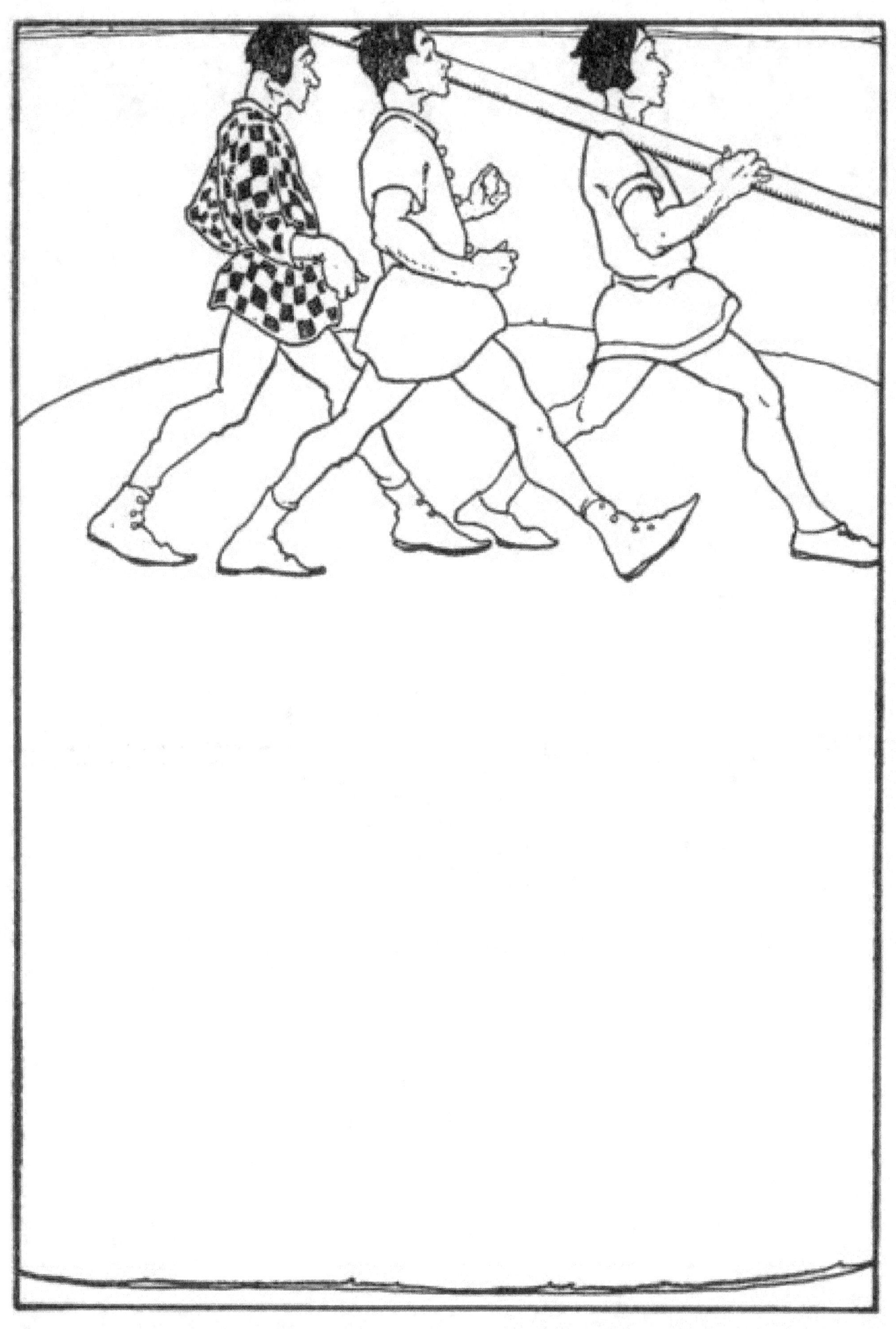

The three friends journeyed on together

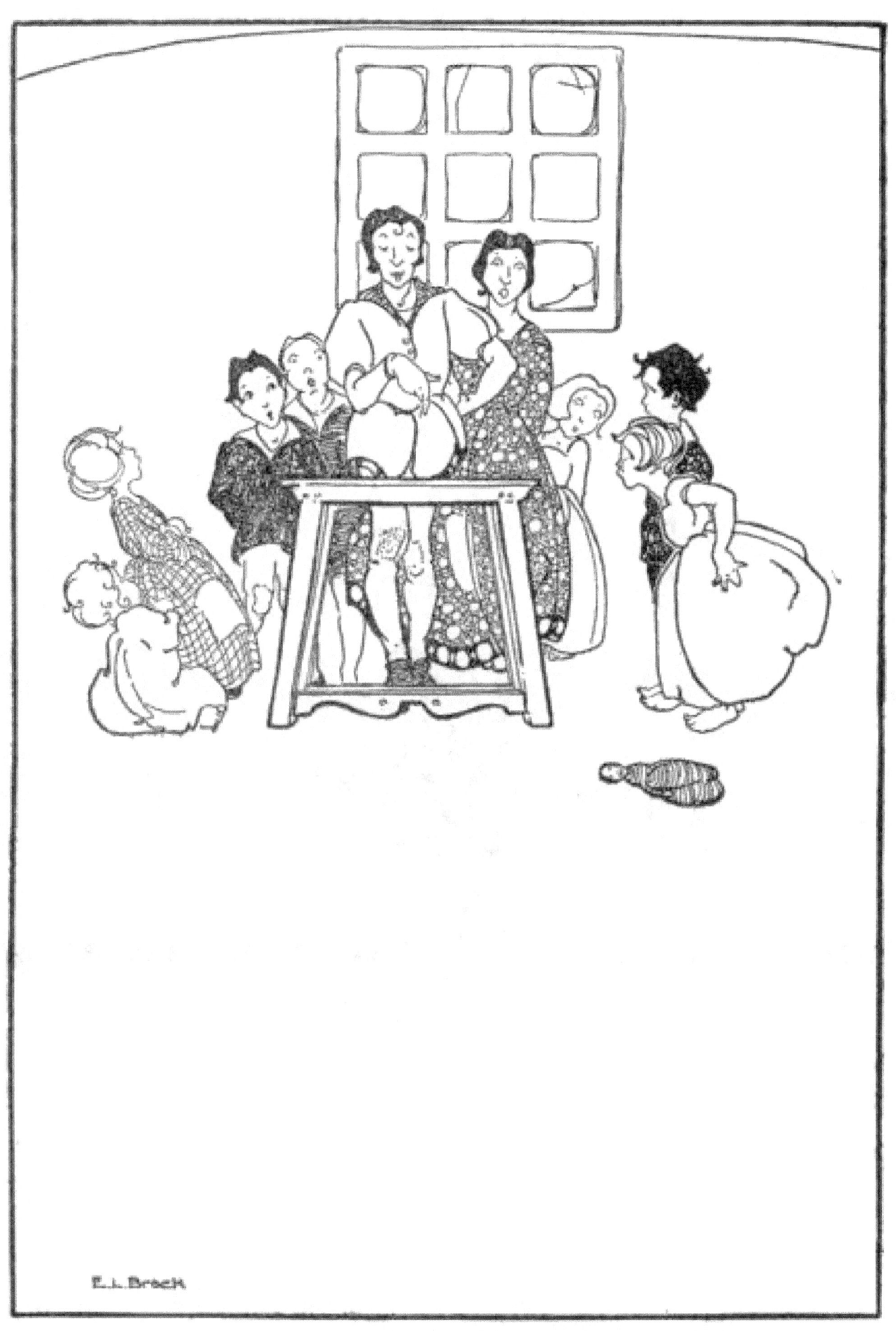

"Table, set yourself," said the man

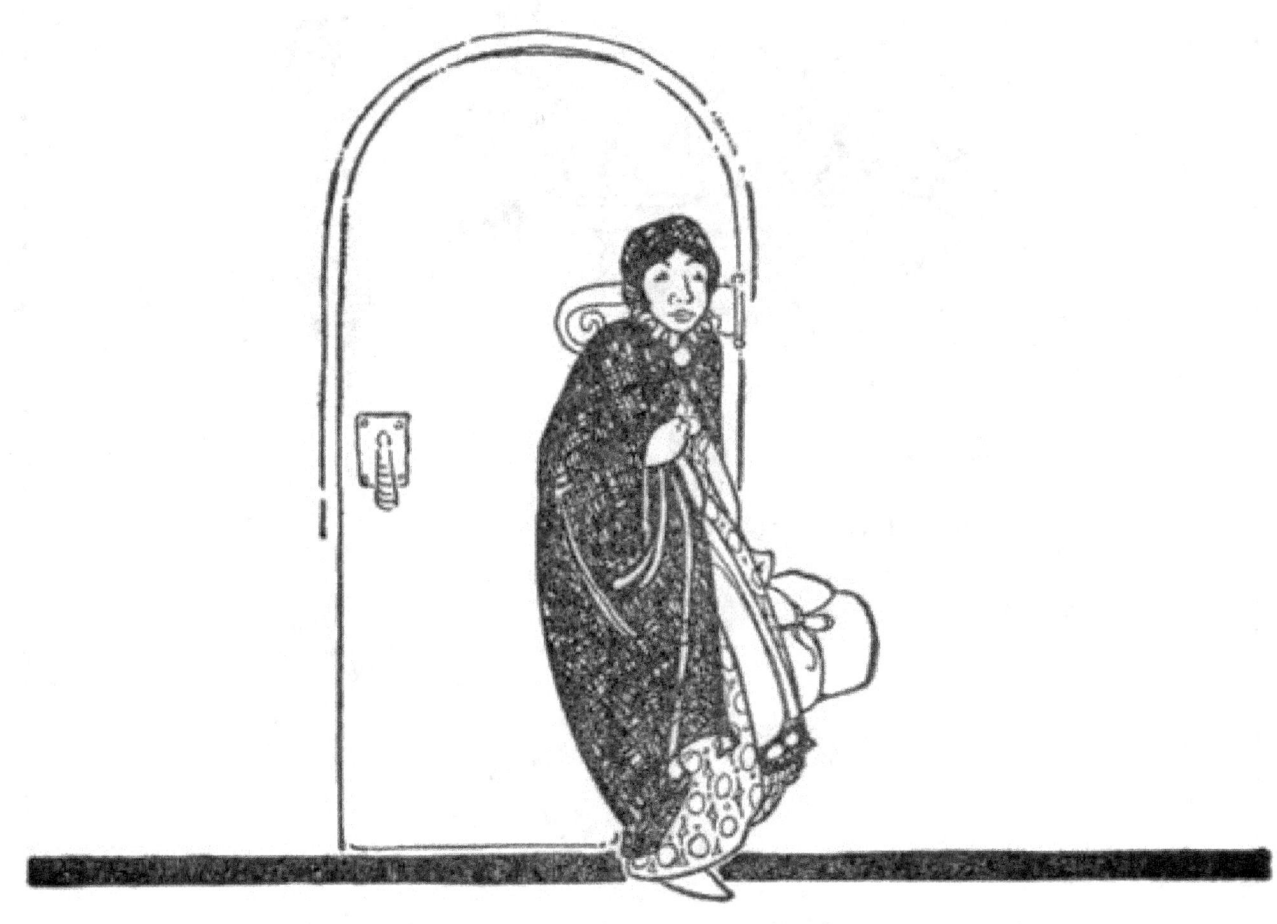

She quietly stole out of the house

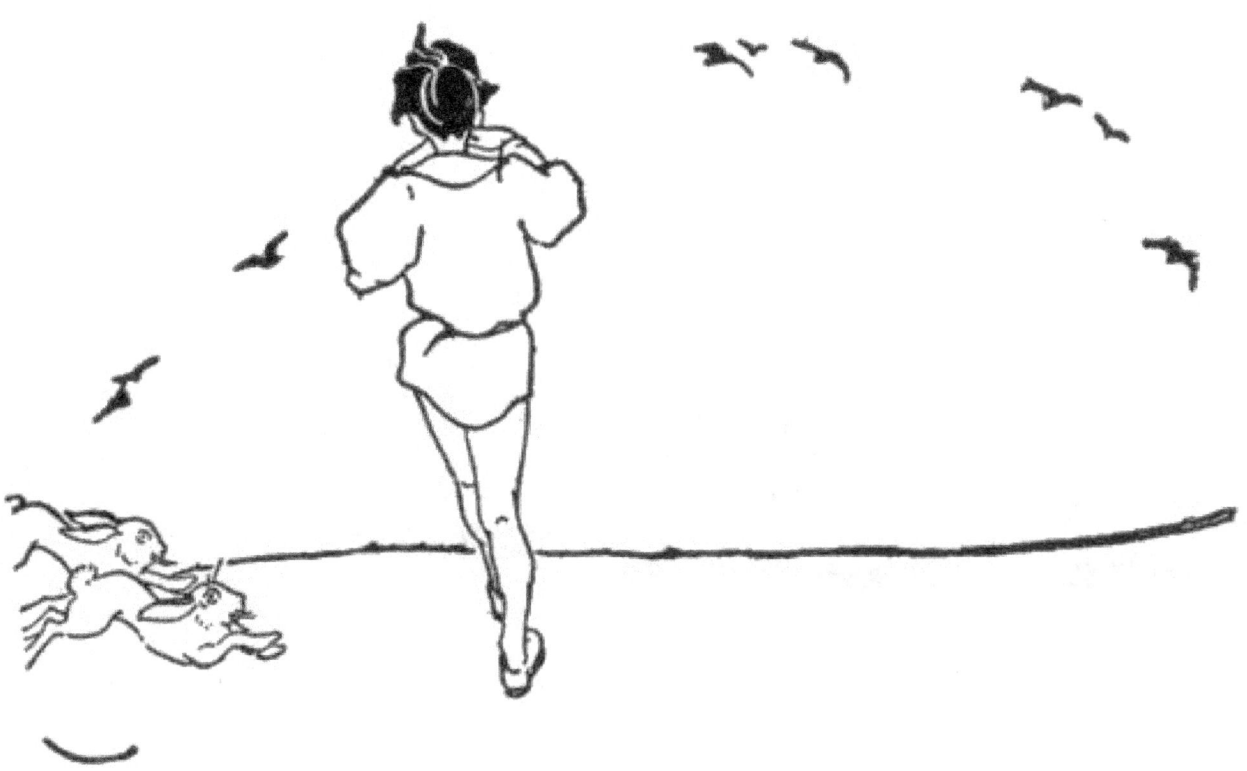

The two rabbits came running up to him

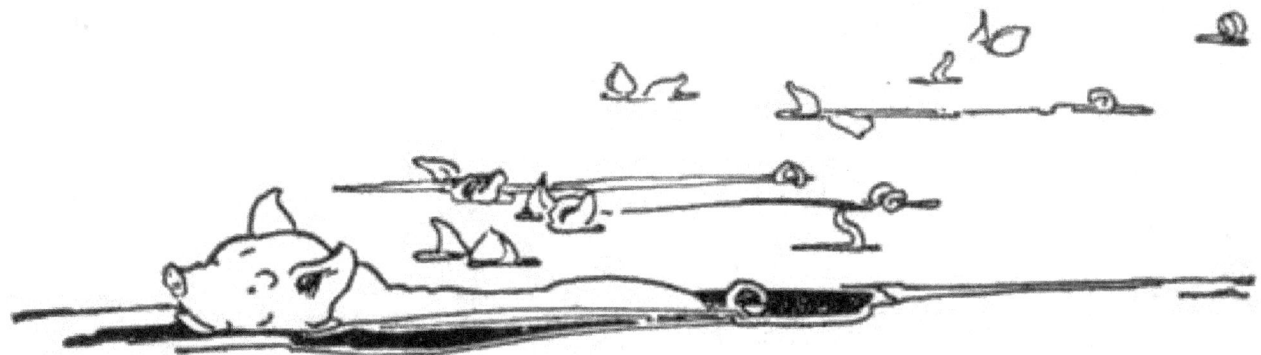

He buried it halfway in the sand

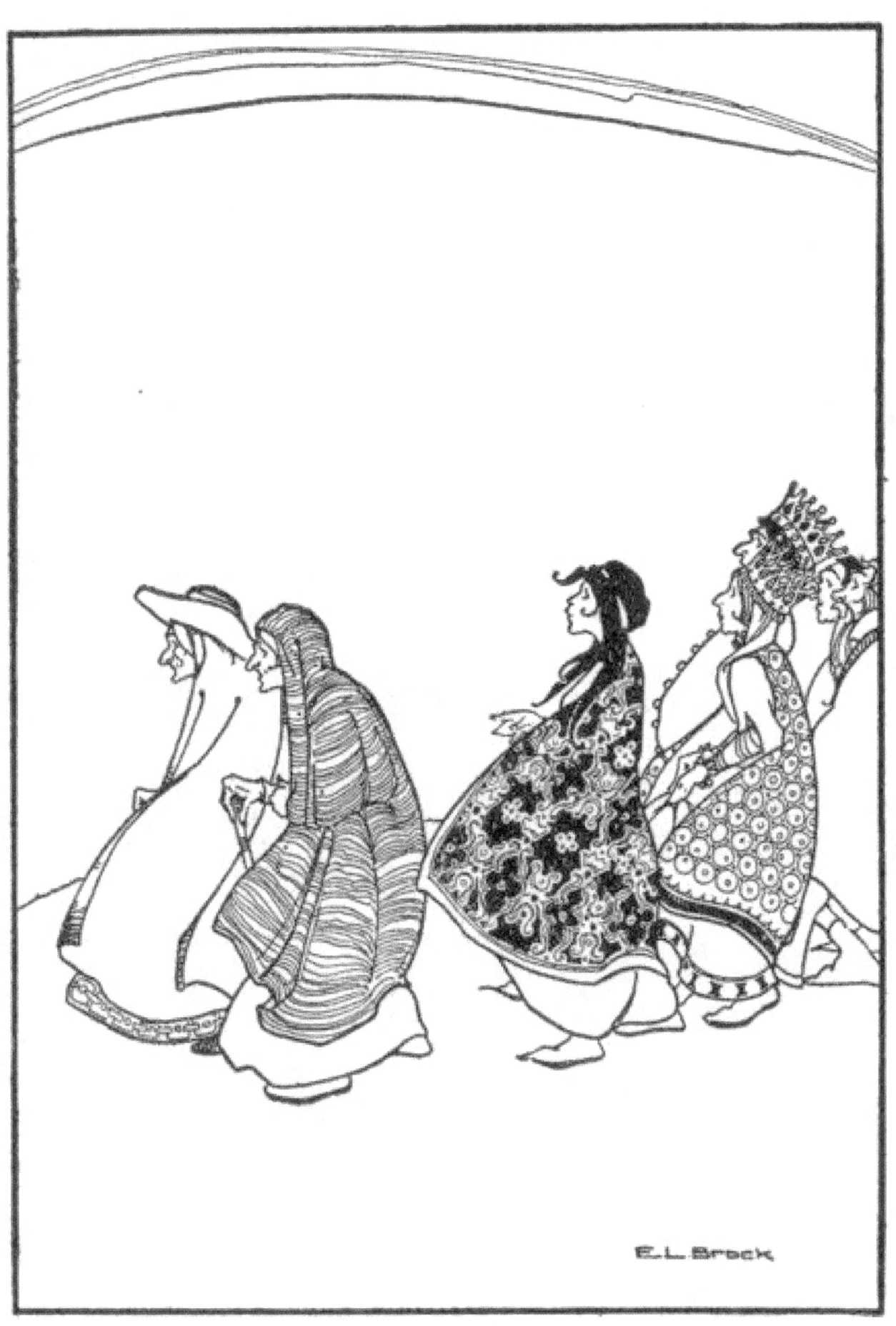

The two old women, the princess, the king and queen, and
all the courtiers followed

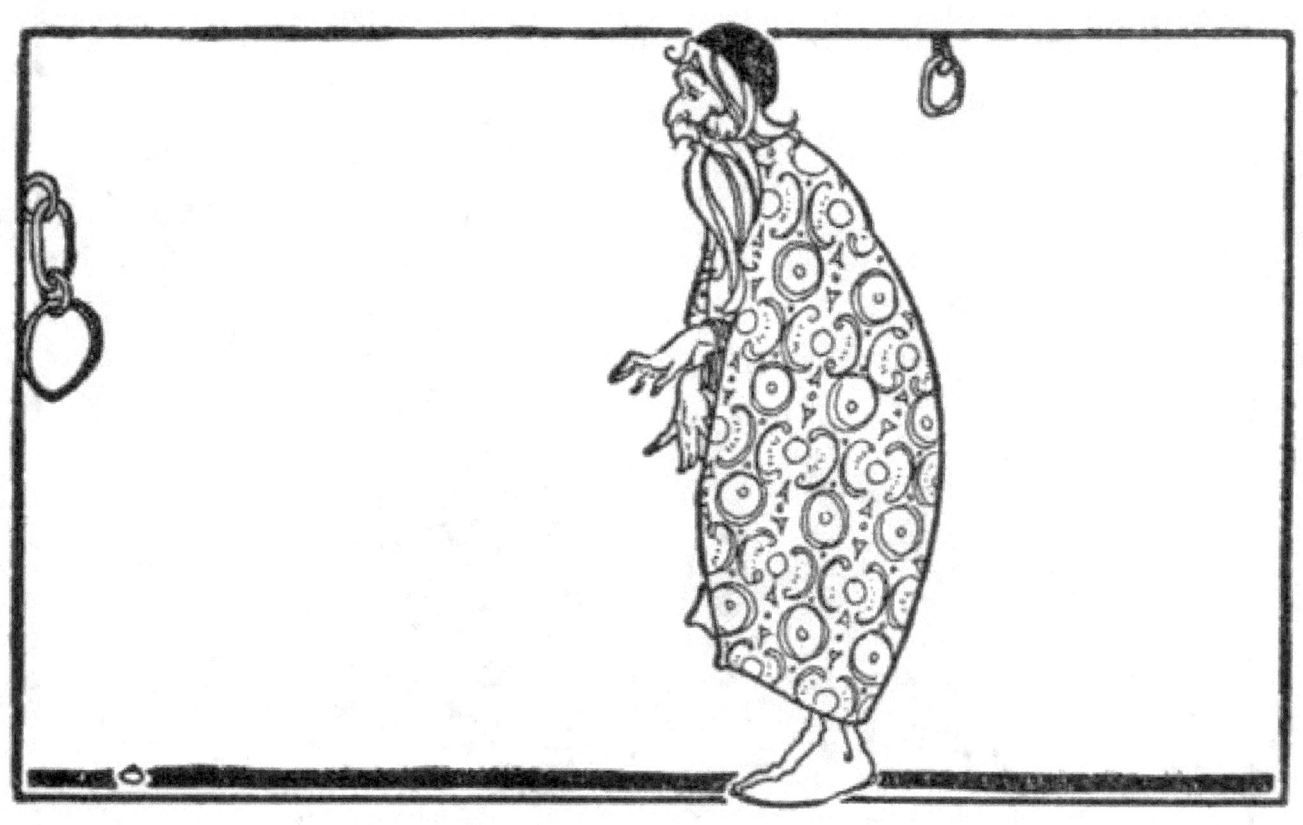

The horse had changed into a kernel of corn

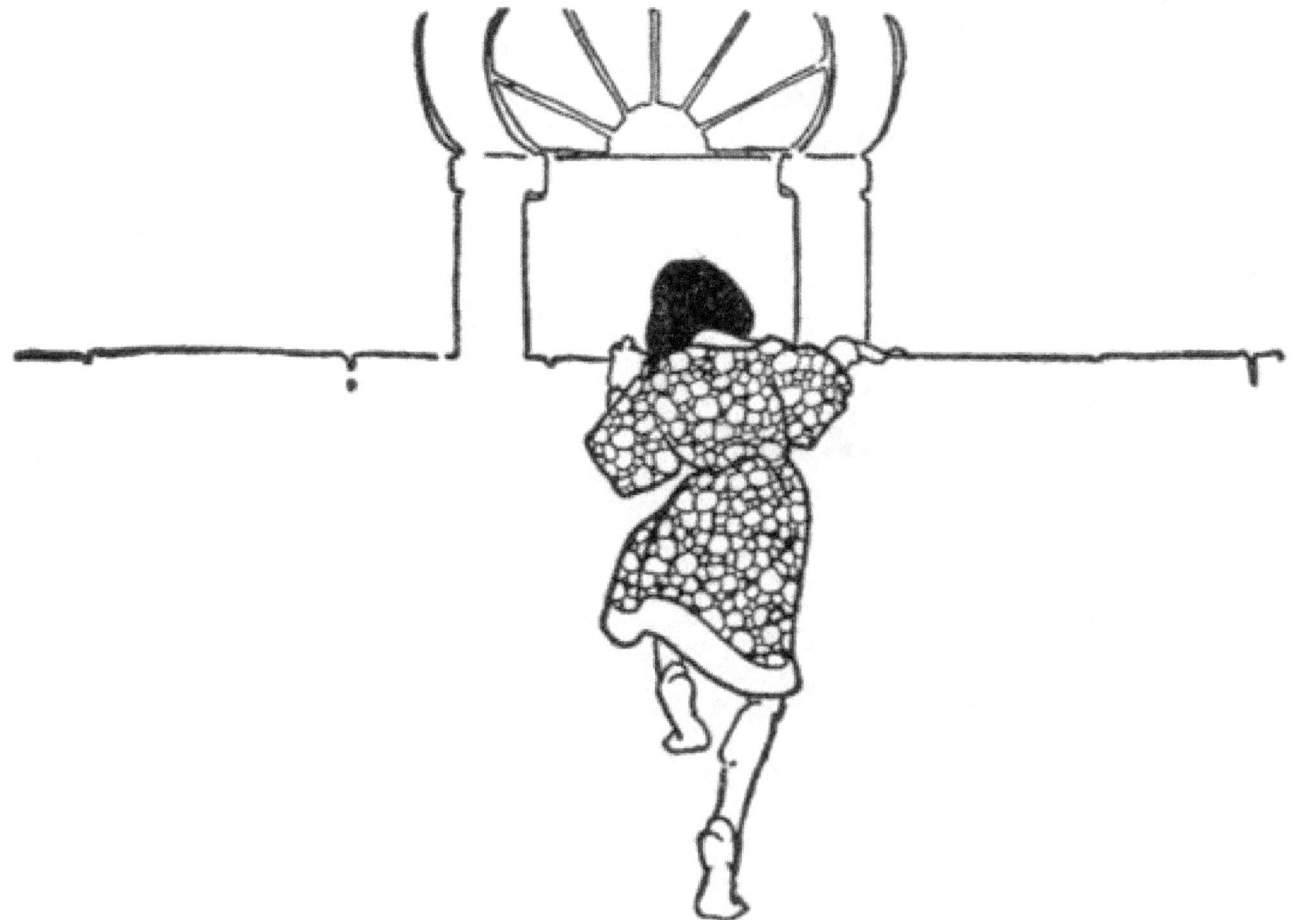

He climbed up the high wall of the palace

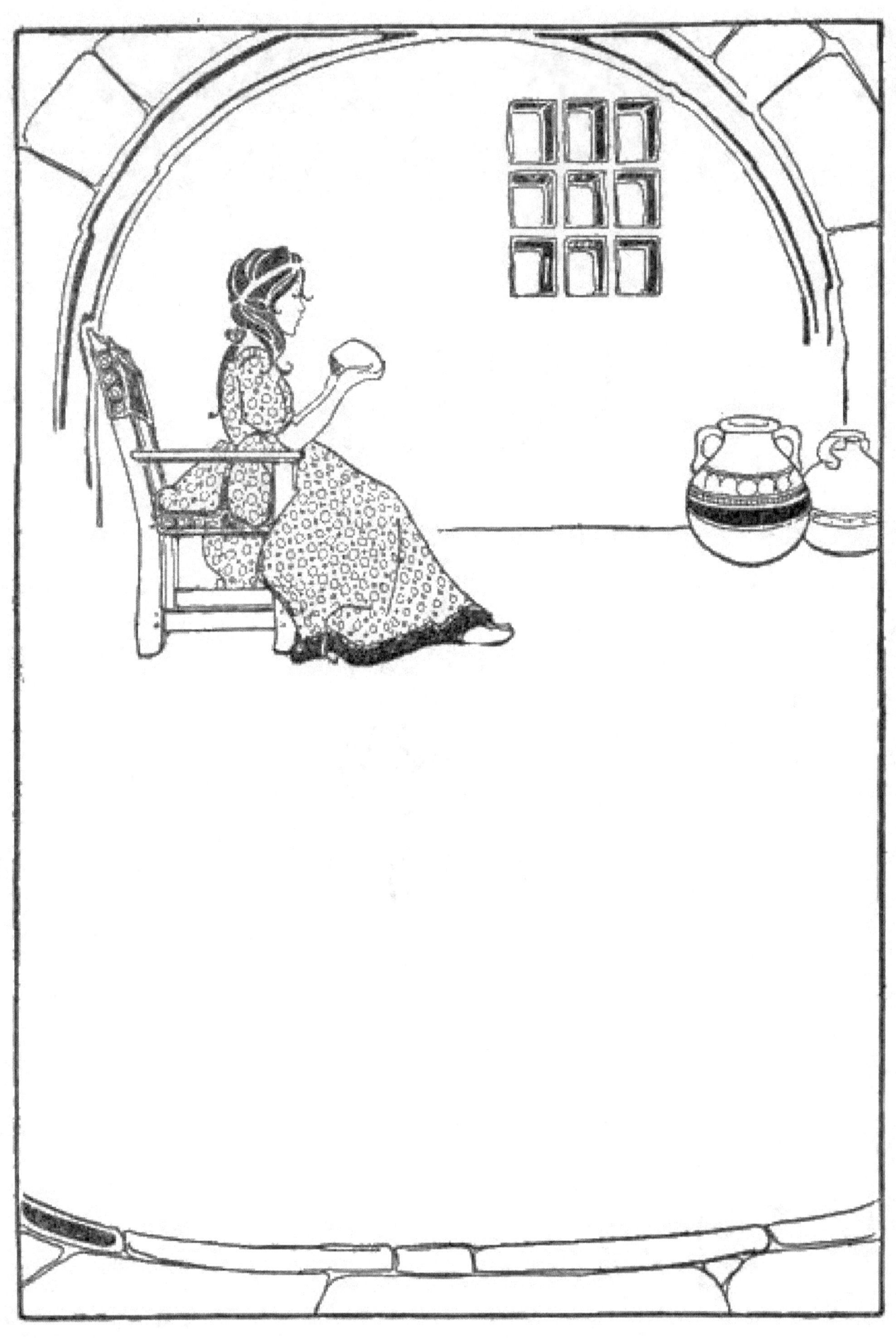

"Oh, stone from my garden wall," she was saying

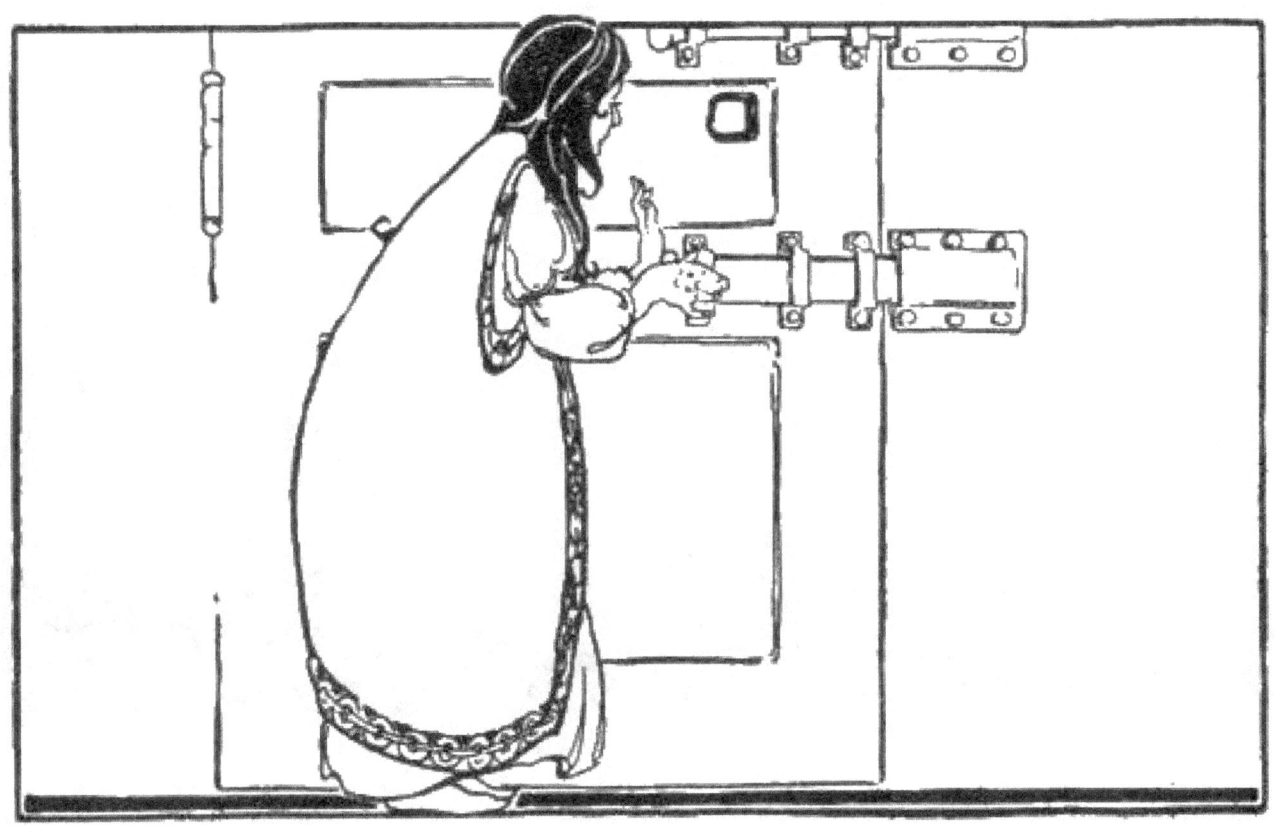

They were big and heavy, but her great fear gave her strength

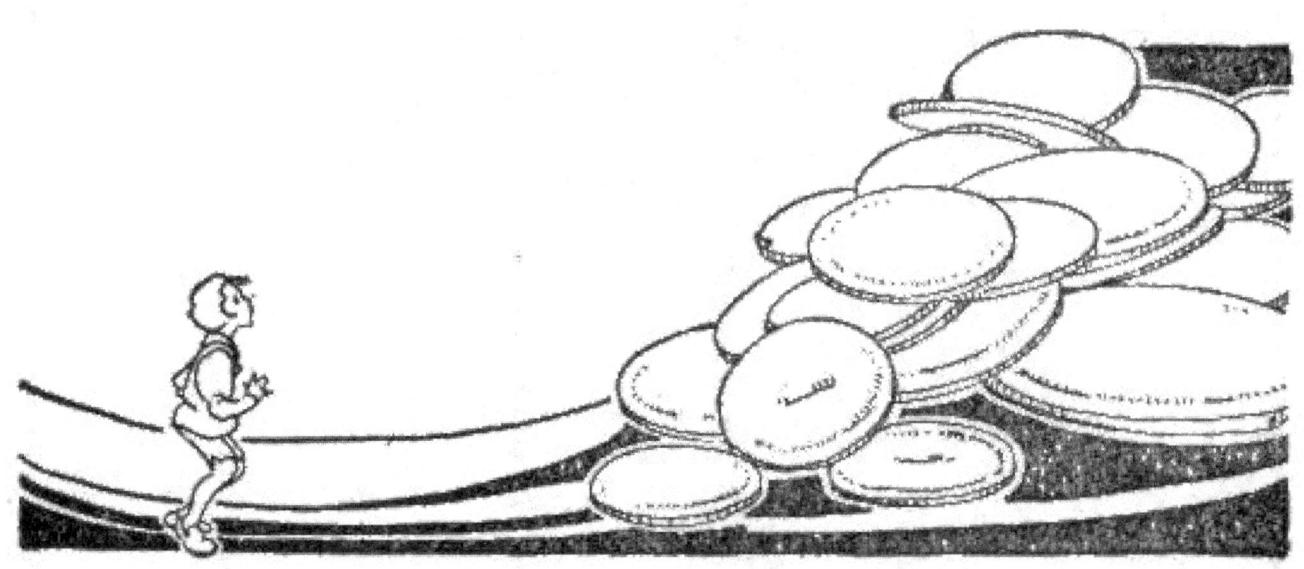

He saw the quantities of gold

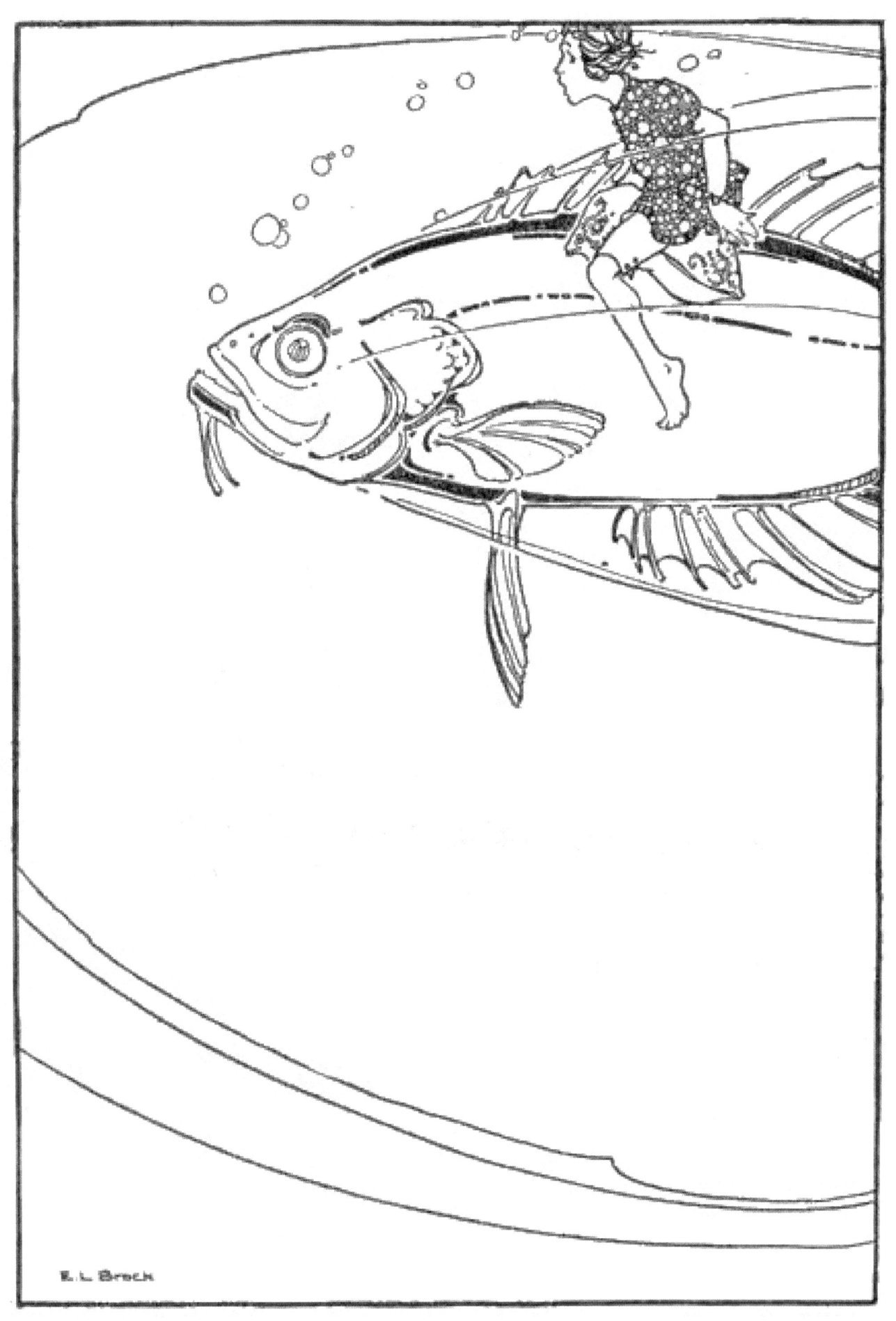

"Take me home as fast as you can!"

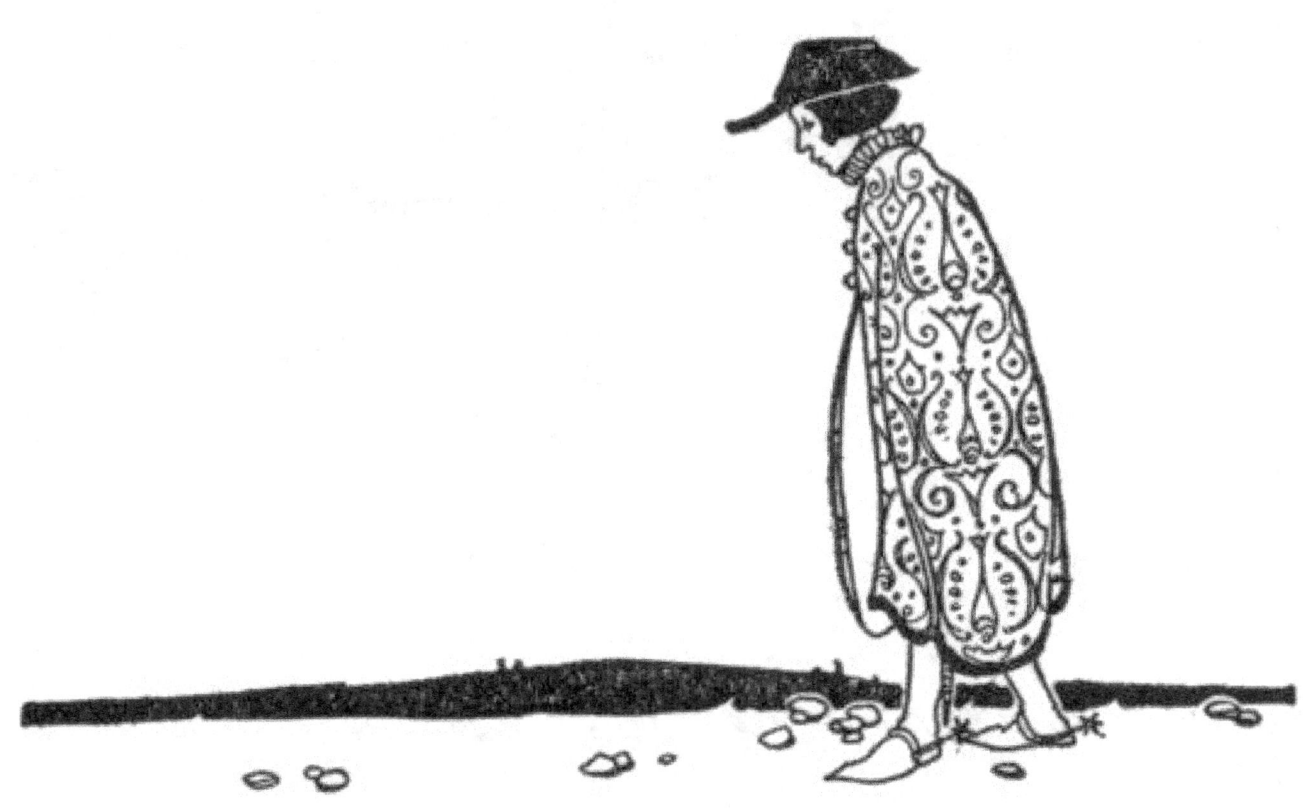

Then he sorrowfully returned to his waiting ship

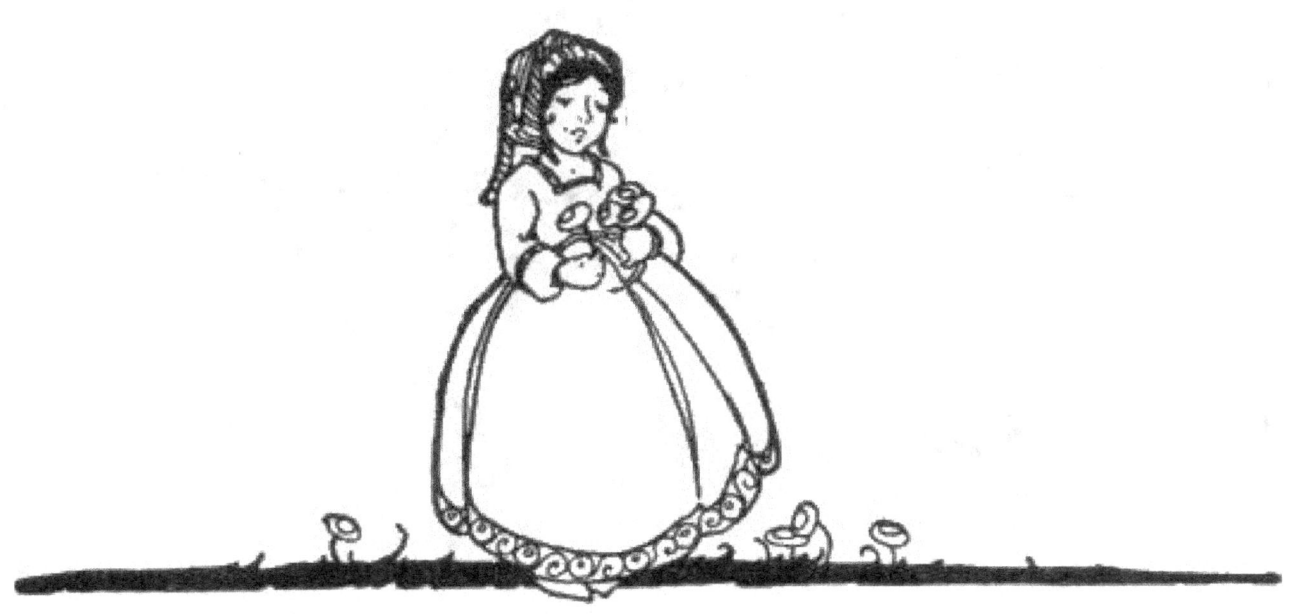

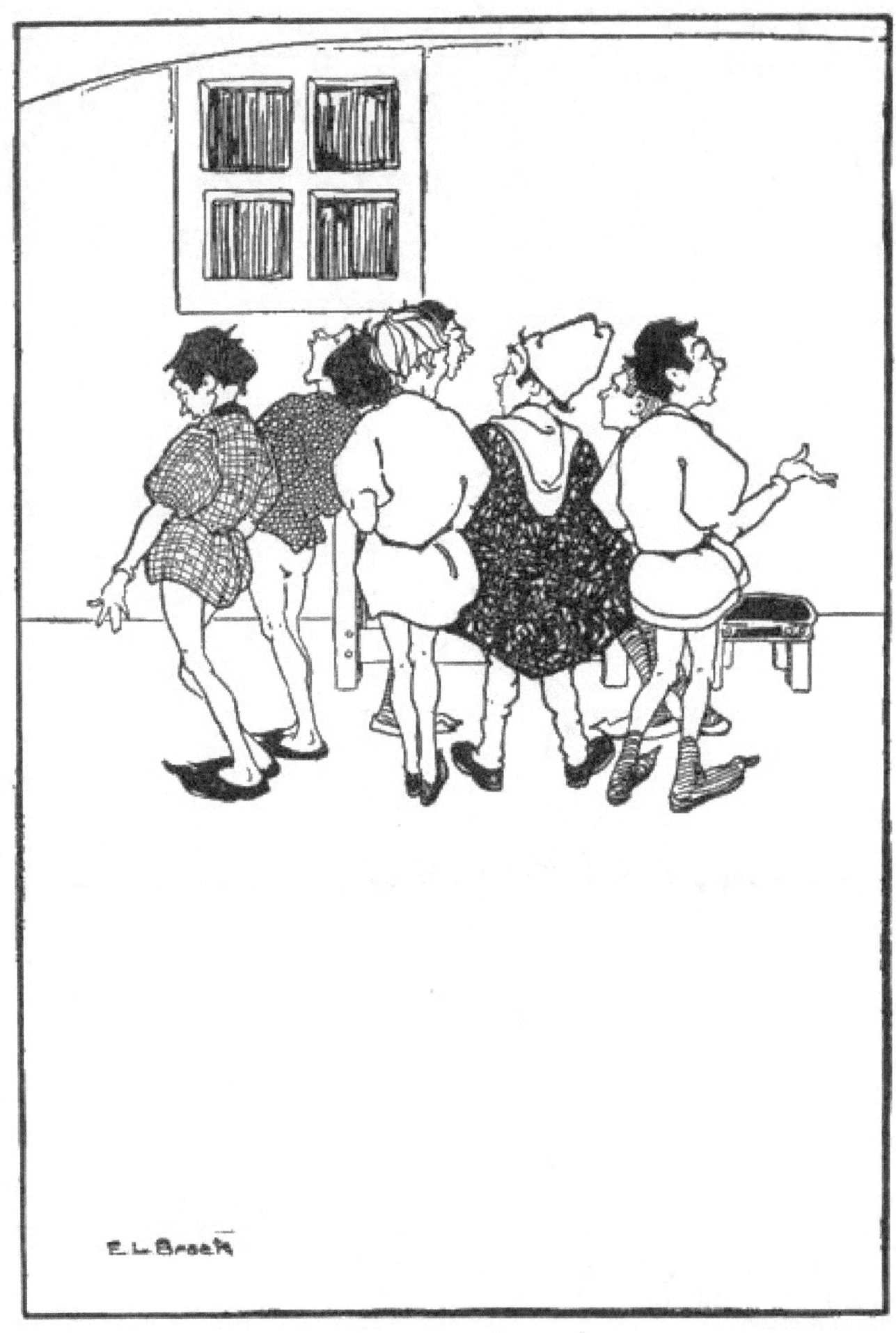

"We never have looked so neat and clean"

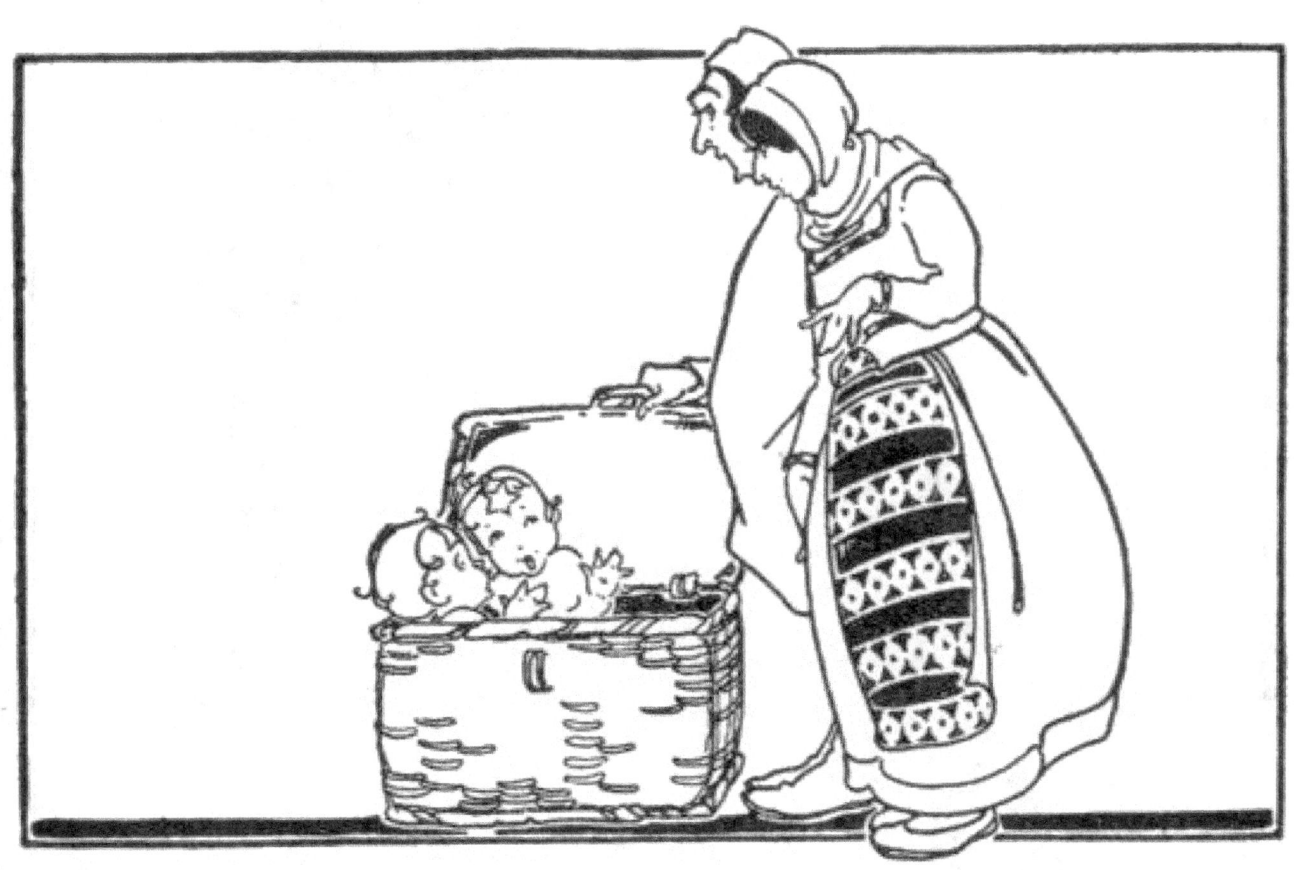

The miller and his wife were the most surprised people in
the whole country

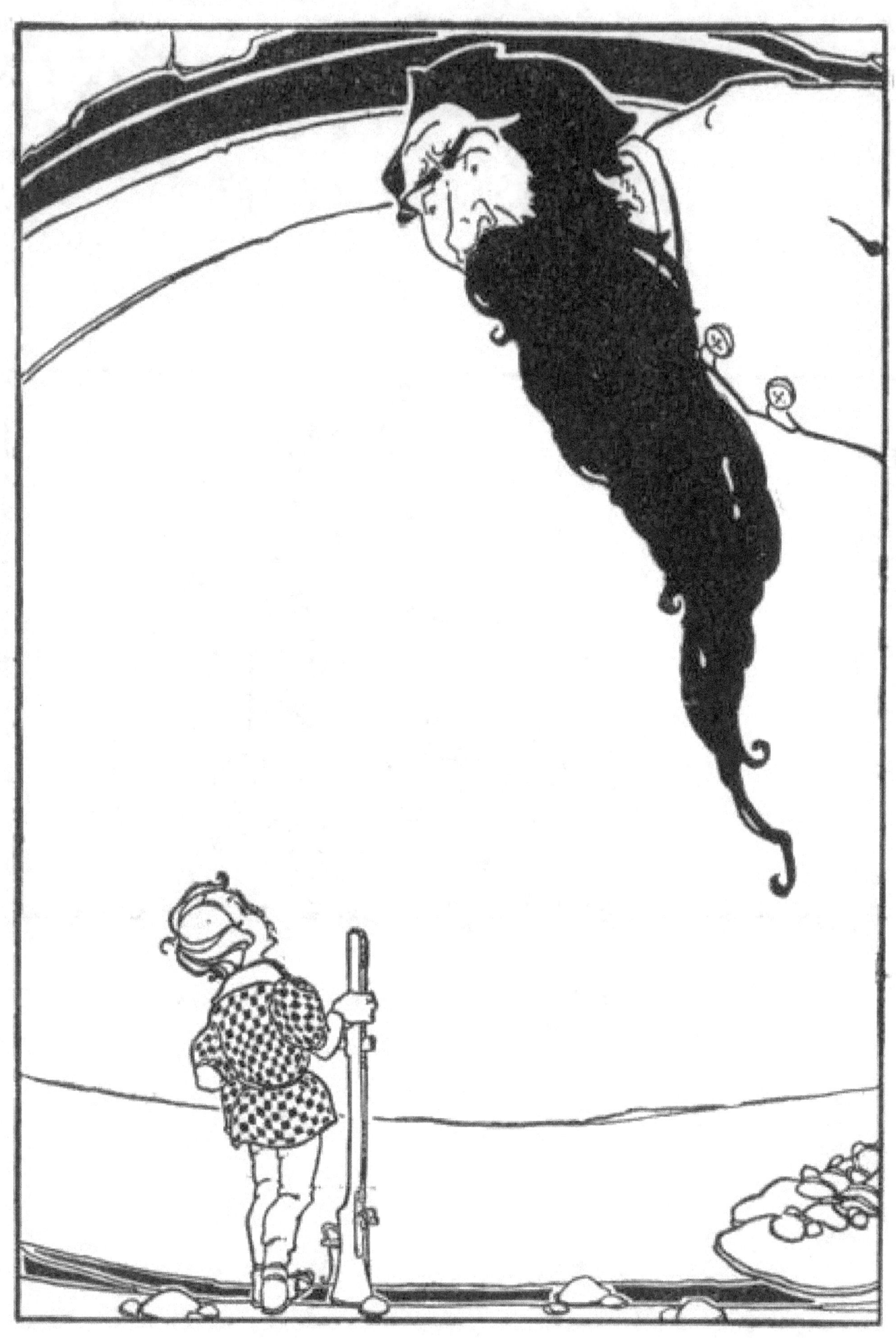

He frowned down at José

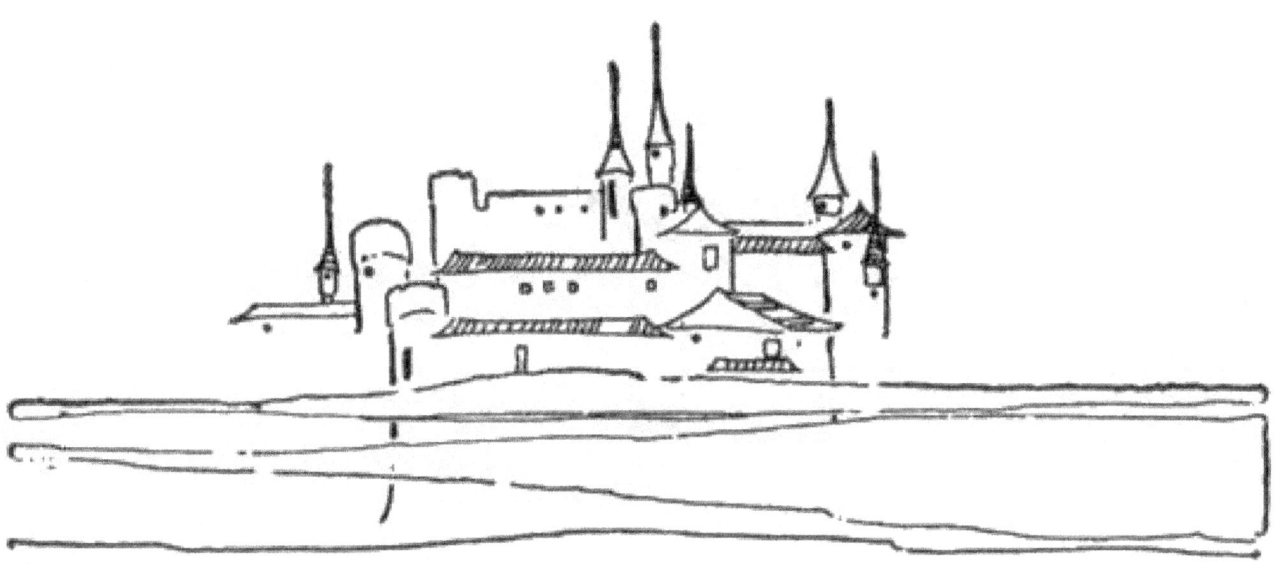

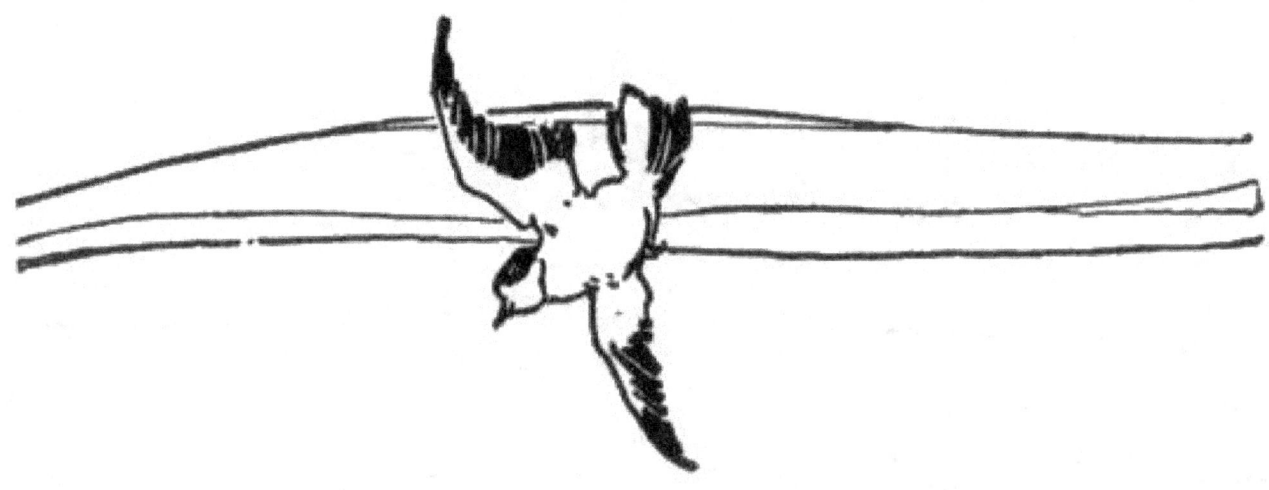

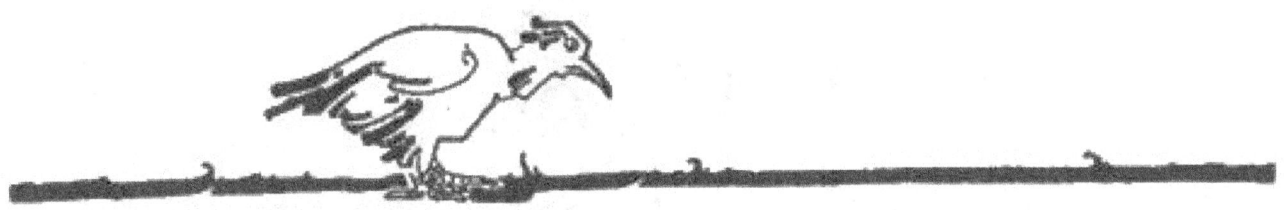

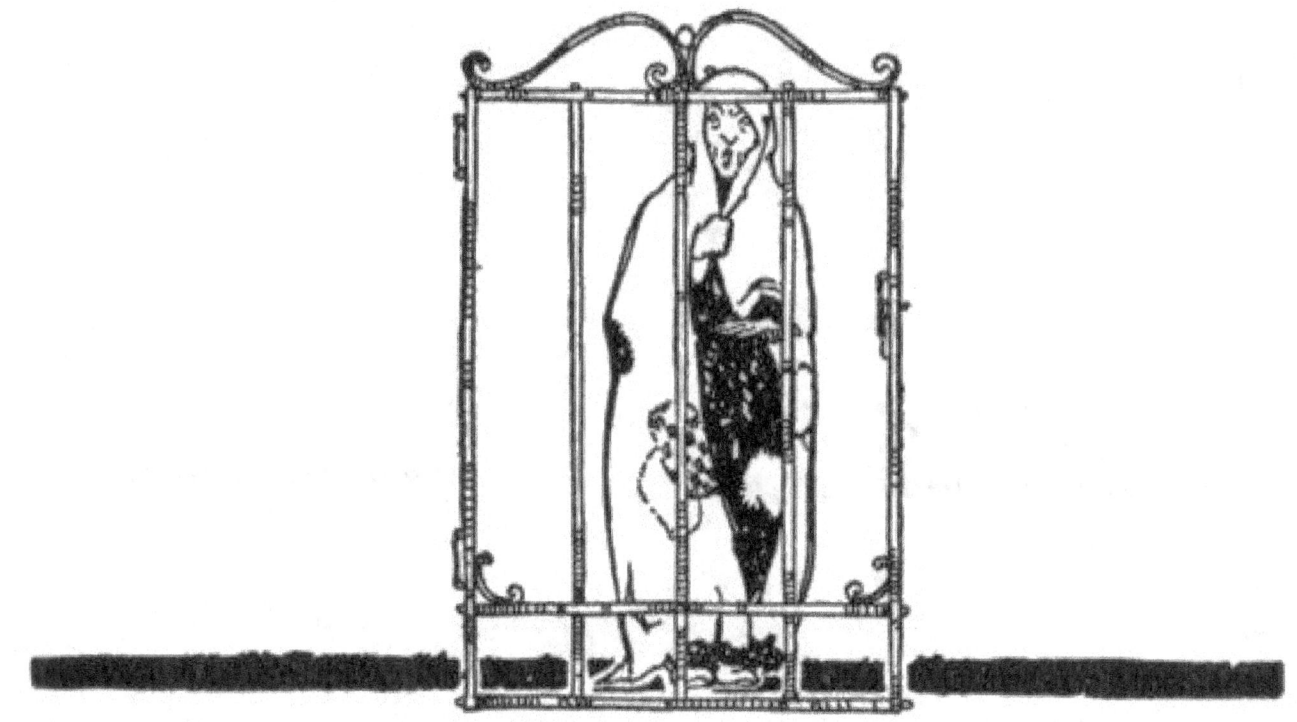

"Alms!  Alms!"

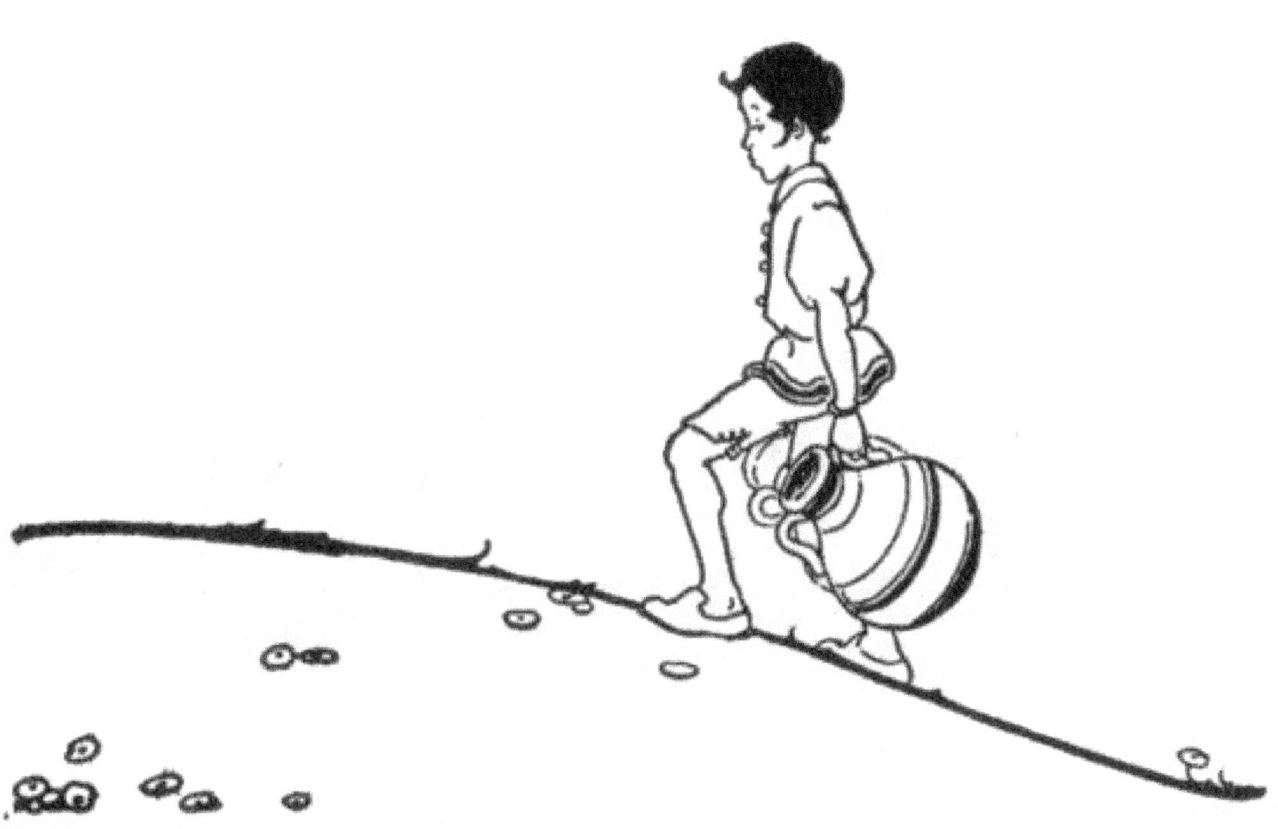

Pedro lifted the two great jars and slowly climbed up the hill

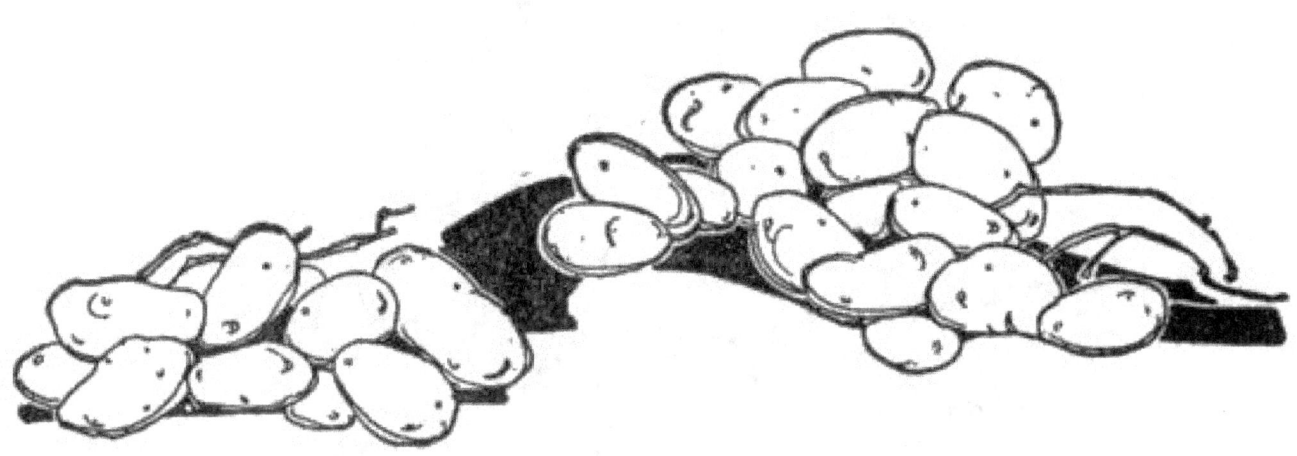

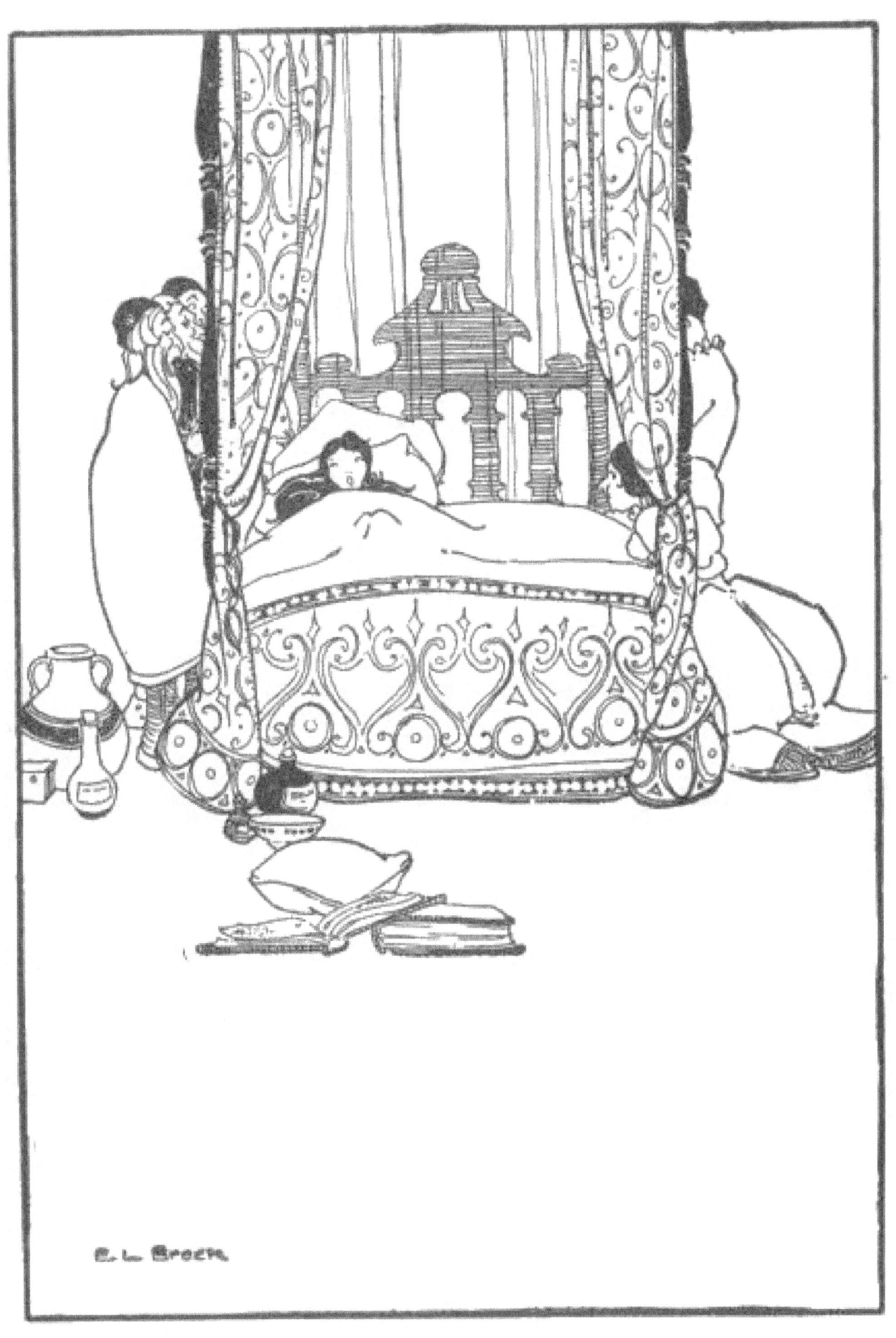

It appeared that the fair maid would die

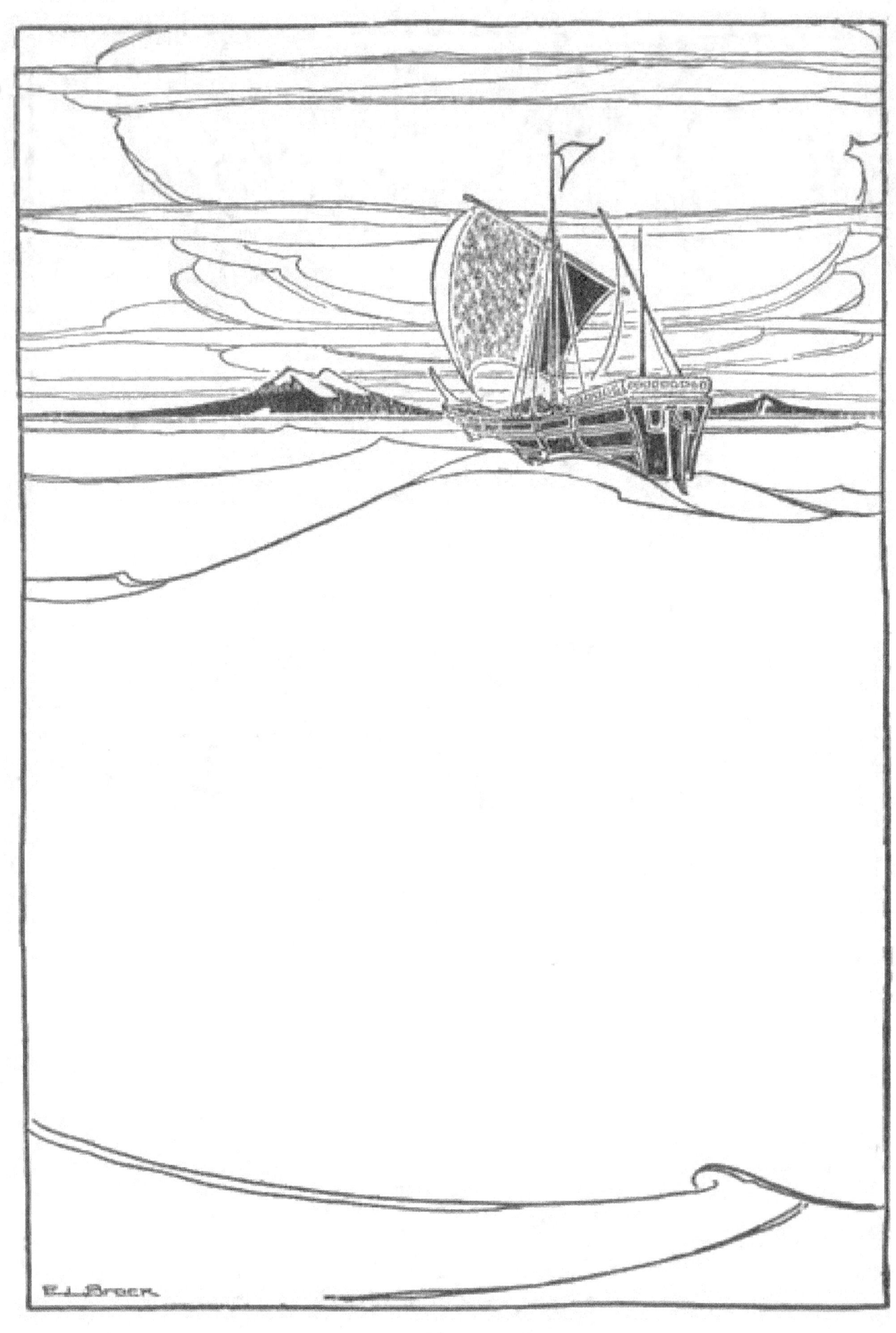

One evening just at sunset

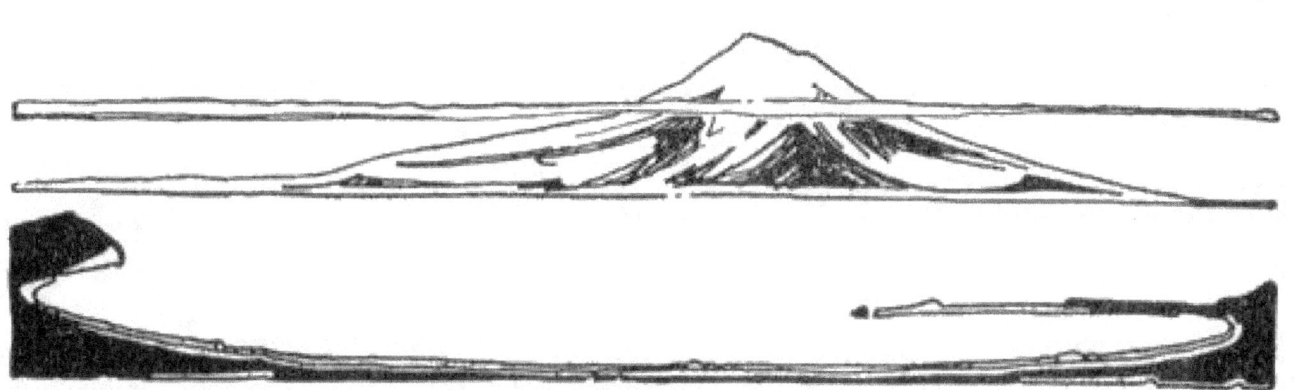

The peaceful snow-capped summit of Mt. Pico

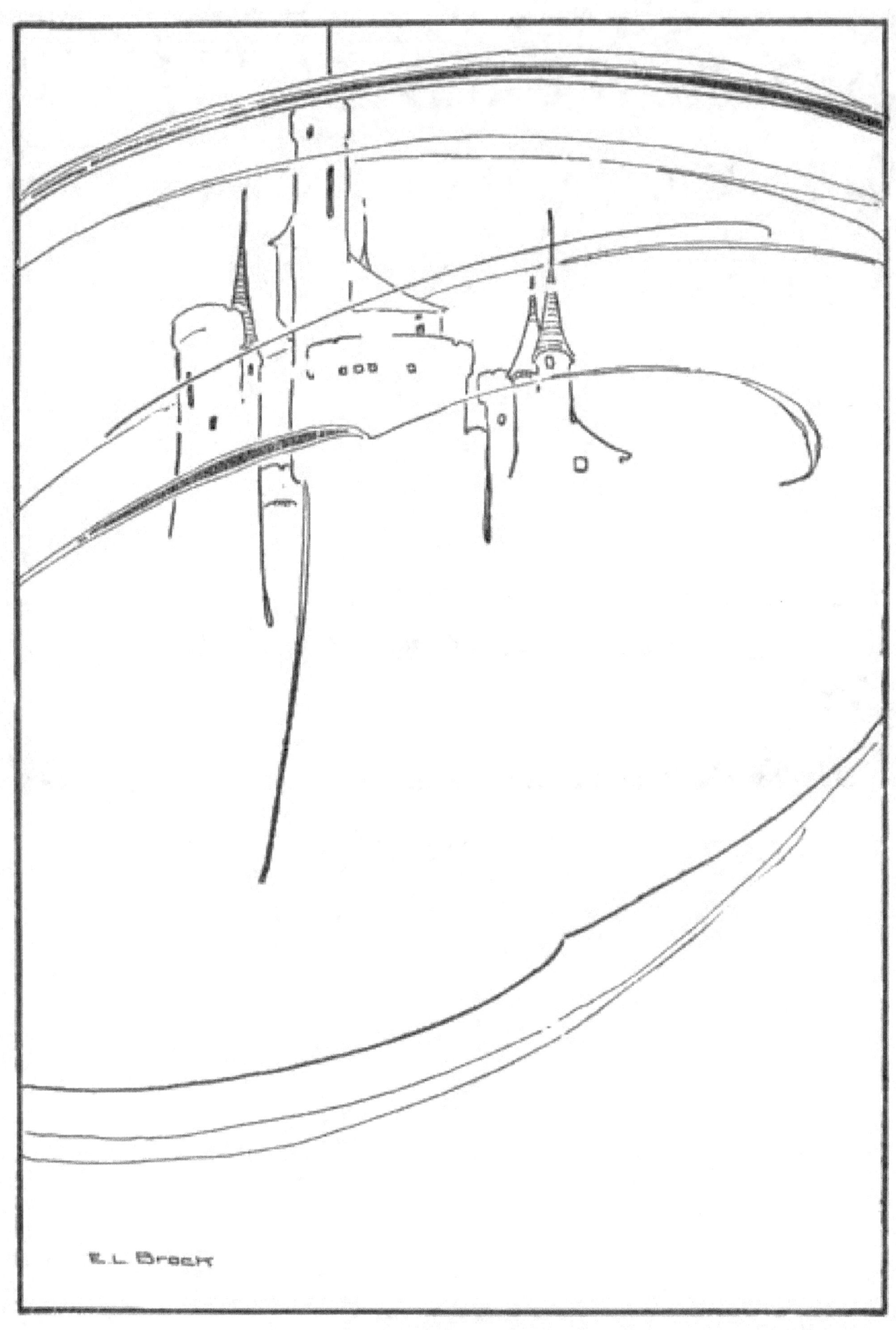

The beautiful enchanted palace in the lake of Ginjal

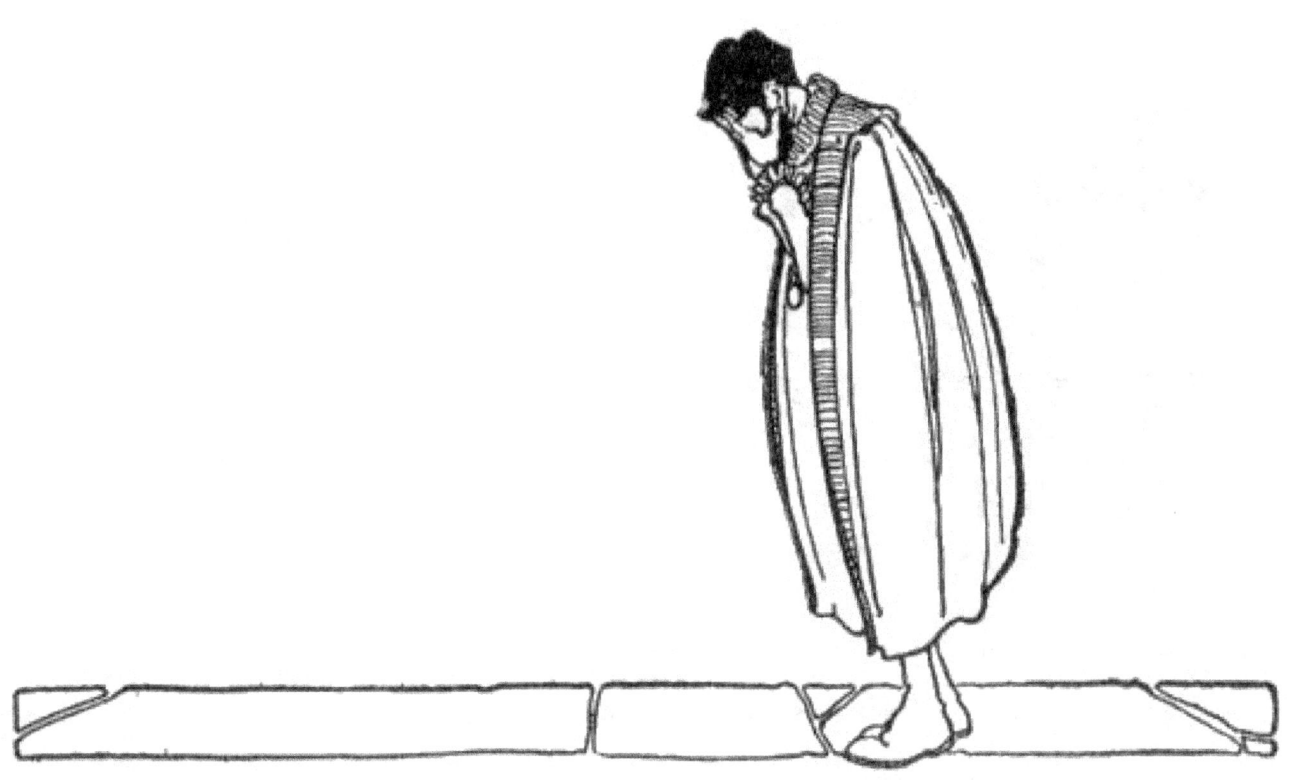

He bowed his head upon his hands

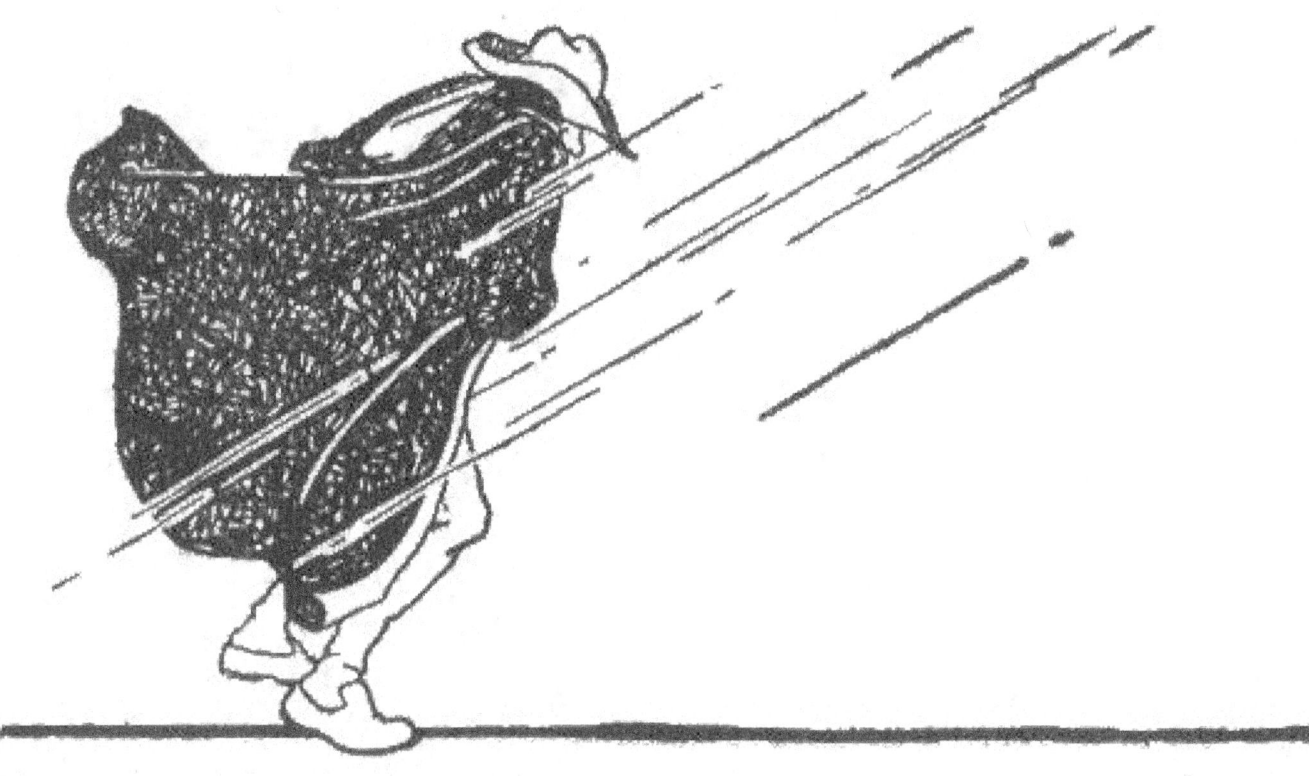

He wrapped himself in the brown cloak and went out
through the fierce blinding storm

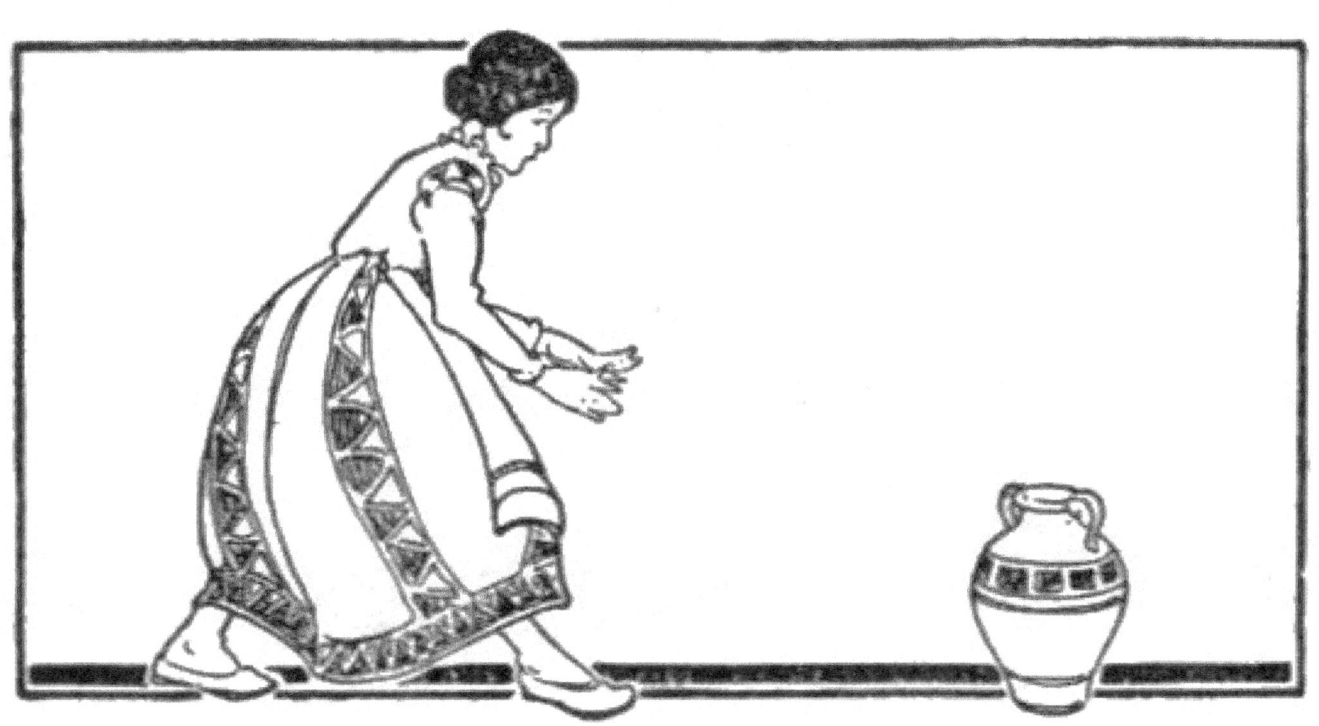

She ran to the water jar

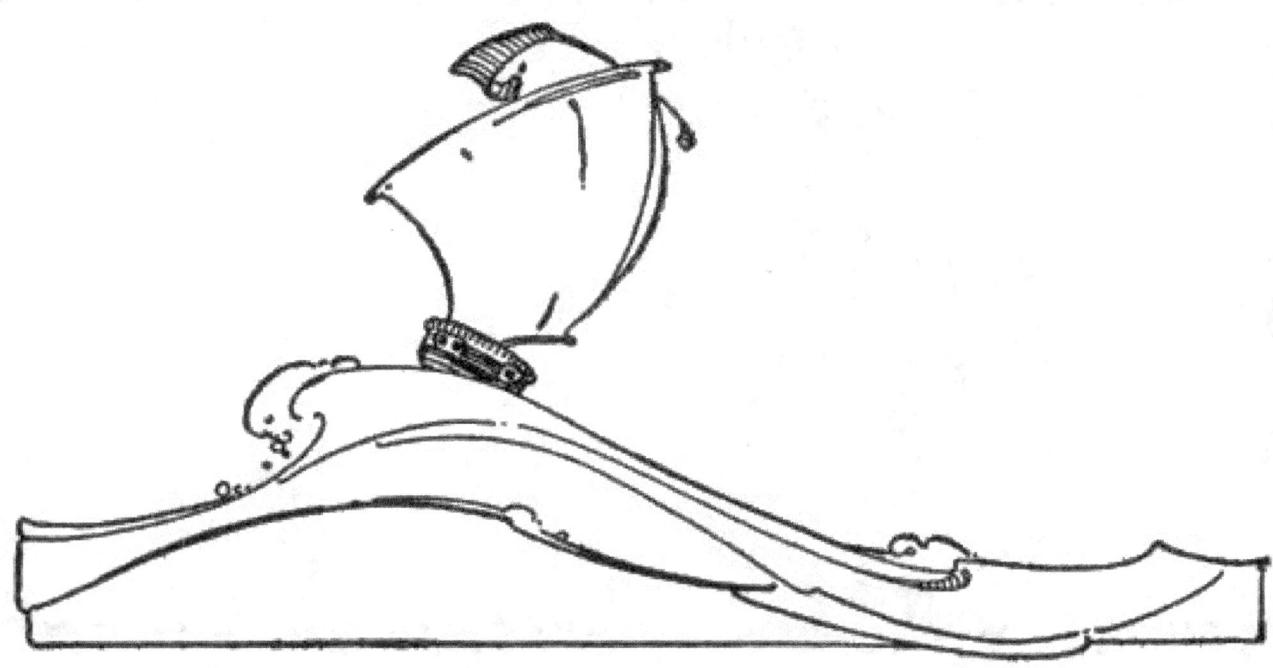

A fierce storm arose

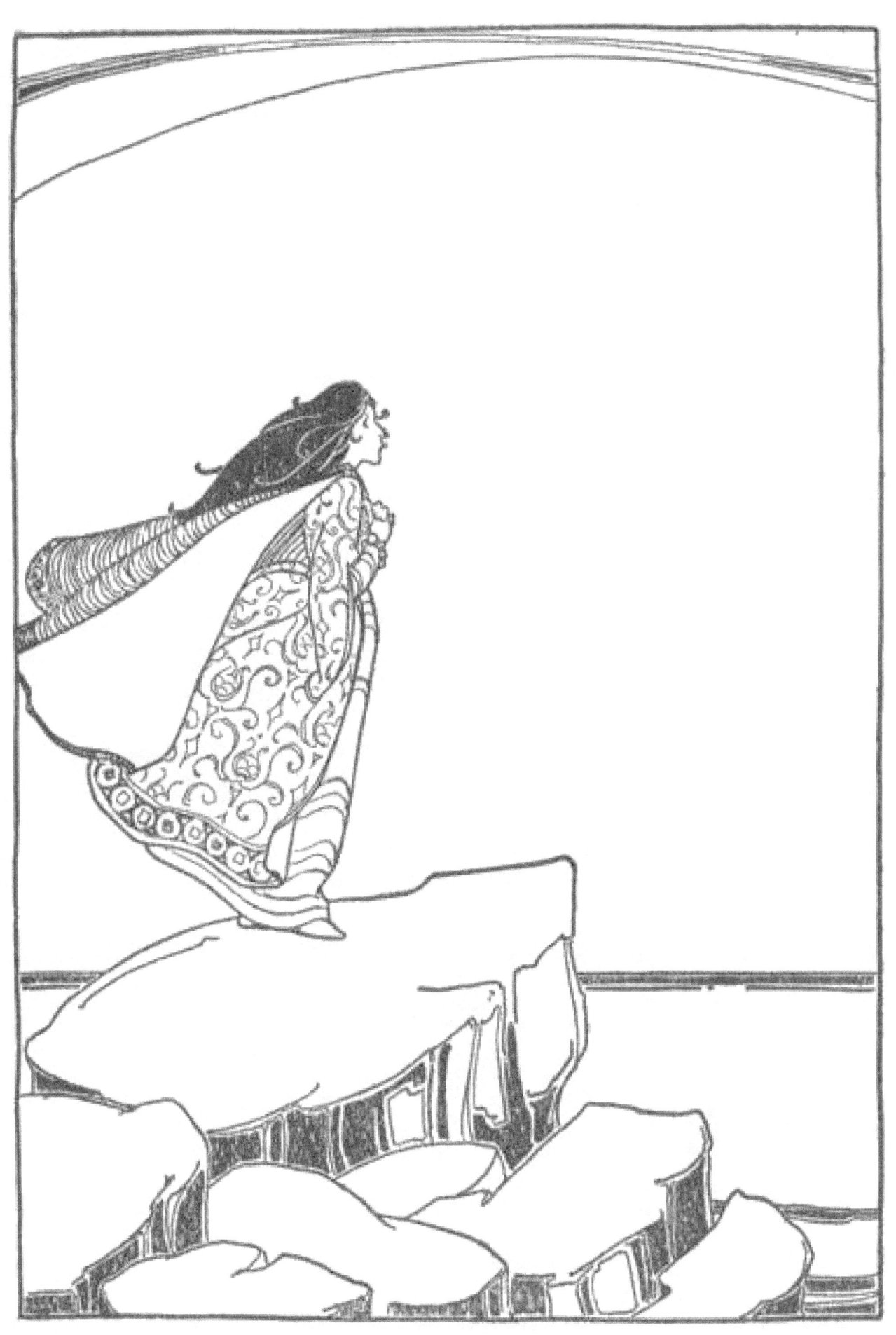

NOTHING BUT THE SEA, SKY AND ROCK